WITHDRAWN

For Reference

Not to be taken from this room

AMERICAN CITIES CHRONOLOGY SERIES

CINCINNATI
A CHRONOLOGICAL & DOCUMENTARY HISTORY

1676-1970

Compiled and Edited by
ROBERT I. VEXLER

Series Editor
HOWARD B. FURER

1975
OCEANA PUBLICATIONS, INC.
Dobbs Ferry, New York

Library of Congress Cataloging in Publication Data

Vexler, Robert I
  Cincinnati: a chronological & documentary history, 1676-1970.

  (American cities chronology series)
  Bibliography: p.
  1. Cincinnati--History--Chronology. 2. Cincinnati --History--Sources. I. Title.
F499.C5V49   1975   977.1'78   74-18044
ISBN 0-379-00603-0

© Copyright 1975 by Oceana Publications, Inc.

All rights reserved. No part of this publication may be reproduced or transmitted in any form or by any means, electronic or mechanical, including photocopy, recording, xerography, or any information storage and retrieval system, without permission in writing from the publisher.

Manufactured in the United States of America

To
David and Melissa

TABLE OF CONTENTS

EDITOR'S FOREWORD. vii

CHRONOLOGY
    Settlement and Early Development, 1676-1801 1
    Incorporation of the City, 1802-1865. 5
    Post Civil War Cincinnati, 1866-1899 31
    The Twentieth Century, 1900-1924 46
    City Manager Form of Government, 1925-1970 52

DOCUMENTS 67
    Inauguration of River Traffic between Cincinnati and
        Pittsburgh, 1794. 68
    Fire Department Regulations, Early Nineteenth Century 70
    Description of Cincinnati, Early Nineteenth Century. 73
    Postal System, Early Nineteenth Century. 76
    Establishment of Cincinnati Water Supply, March 31, 1817. . . 79
    Antislavery Controversy, 1836 81
    City Purchase of Water Works, March 16, 1839. 86
    Cincinnati in 1840 87
    Regulations for Gas Lighting, June 16, 1841 89
    Recommendations for Improvement of Navigation around the
        Falls of the Ohio River, 1846 92
    Revised City Charter, 1850. 95
    City Charter, November 2, 1926 98
    First City Manager's Report, January 5, 1927 101
    The Spirit of the New Cincinnati, May 1928. 103
    Report on the Citizen's Charter Committee, September 1934 . . 106
    The Master Plan, March 1946. 113
    Report on Recreation, December 1947. 117
    The Metropolitan Master Plan, Adopted November 22, 1948 . . 122
    Central Business District Circulation System, January 1957 . . 128
    Cincinnati Ethical Code, December 1963. 131
    Riot after Martin Luther King Funeral, April 8, 1968 133
    Anti-Riot Ordinance, April 17, 1968. 135

BIBLIOGRAPHY 139
    Primary Sources 139
    Secondary Sources. 142
    Articles 148

NAME INDEX. 151

EDITOR'S FOREWORD

    Every effort has been made to cite the most accurate dates in the chronology. Various newspapers, documents, letters, and chronicles have been consulted to determine exact dates. Later scholarship has been used to verify this information or to change dates when proven more plausible.
    Because the very nature of preparing a chronology of this type precludes the author from using the standard form of historical footnoting, I should like to acknowledge in this editor's foreword the major sources used to compile the bulk of the chronological and factual materials comprising the chronology section of this work. They are as follows: Charles Frederick Goss, <u>Cincinnati, The Queen City, 1788-1912</u>, 4 vols.; Charles T. Greve, <u>Centennial History of Cincinnati and Representative Citizens</u>; Lewis Alexander Leonard, ed., <u>Greater Cincinnati and Its People: A History</u>, 4 vols.; Zane L. Miller, <u>Boss Cox's Cincinnati: Urban Politics in the Progressive Era</u>; and Richard C. Wade, <u>The Urban Frontier</u>.
    This research tool is compiled primarily for the student. The importance of political, social, economic, and cultural events has been evaluated in relation to their significance for the development of Cincinnati as one of the major cities, included in this series, that have contributed to the growth of America. Cincinnati has played a major role in the development of the United States. Its citizens early recognized the fine location of the city in relation to the Middle West and encouraged the development of its commercial and industrial potential. After having been involved in the era of the political boss and the ensuing corruption, Cincinnati was to develop an experimental type of government in the twentieth century: the city-manager form of municipal governance. Cincinnati also early initiated a program of urban planning and redevelopment, which contributed to its ability to retain and improve its economic position.
    Documents have been selected that best illustrate the major aspects in the development of Cincinnati from the small early American town to the bustling and growing city of the 1960s.

                                          Robert I. Vexler, Ph.D.
                                          Briarcliff College

CHRONOLOGY

SETTLEMENT AND EARLY DEVELOPMENT

1676   May 17. Marquette and Joliet began their voyage that resulted in the discovery of the Mississippi.

1763   October 7. By proclamation, the territory including that of Ohio was reserved by King George III for the Indians as hunting grounds.

1768   By the Treaty of Stanwix the Indians recognized the Ohio River as the boundary between the white men and themselves.

1786   March. The Ohio Company was founded by Gen. Rufus Putnam, Gen. Samuel H. Parsons, and Rev. Manasseh Cutler. They selected a site around the Muskingum River. The grant was signed October 27.

1787   August 29. Benjamin Stites and John Cleves Symmes petitioned Congress for a grant on the same terms as the Ohio Company.

1788   August 5. Matthias Denman, Col. Robert Patterson, and John Filson signed an agreement as to the rights and duties for their contemplated enterprise in the Northwest Territory.

September 22. A large company of Kentuckians with Col. Patterson and Filson landed and were met by Judge Symmes, who had come from Limestone.

November 18. Benjamin Stites and a band of companions founded the settlement of Columbia at the mouth of the Little Miami River.

December 28. A group of settlers landed in Yeatman's Cove in what was to become Cincinnati.

December 29. The pioneers under Matthias Denman broke up their boats to construct their houses at Losantiville (Cincinnati).

1789   Gen. Arthur St. Clair was appointed governor of the Northwest Territory when it was founded. He was removed by Jefferson in 1802.

William McMillan was chosen judge and John Ludlow sheriff.

January 3. John Cleves Symmes took a letter of friendship to the Indians.

January 7. A drawing took place for the donation lots after Israel Ludlow and others had completed their survey of the town.

February 2. John Cleves Symmes and his followers landed at North Bend.

May. A large number of lots were given away to newcomers.

August 20. The site for Fort Washington was decided upon.

1790   The first courthouse was built.

January 2. Governor St. Clair arrived at Fort Washington.

January 4. Governor St. Clair promulgated Hamilton County. The governor also changed the name of the town from Losantiville to Cincinnati in honor of the Society of the Cincinnati (Revolutionary War Officers), which had been formed May 13, 1783.

January 5. The governor ordered the newly appointed justices of the peace to set up the administration of justice.

February 2. The court sat for a brief session. It sat again in May for a longer and more important term.

September 26. General Harmar led troops out of Cincinnati to deal with the Indians. They found the villages deserted 172 miles from Cincinnati and burned them. The Indians then attacked and were able to repel the troops.

October 16. The Presbyterian church was formally organized by Rev. David Rice.

1791   Robert Shaw, known as the "water witch," dug the first well in Cincinnati.

1792   The first school was established in Cincinnati.

February 18. A proclamation was issued empowering Robert Benham to run a ferry over the Ohio River.

July 16. Benjamin Lincoln, Beverly Randolph, and Timothy Pickering represented the government in Detroit, where they received an ultimatum from the sixteen nations that the Ohio River should be the boundary between the United States and the Indians.

1793   The first jail was erected.

James White taught night school four evenings each week for three months at $2.00 "per" student.

R. Haughton taught minuet, cotillions, country dances, and Scotch reels.

Griffin Yeatman built the first log tavern.

Dr. Richard Allison, surgeon at the garrison, answered calls for citizens and settled in the village after the fort was abandoned.

Spring. The Baptist church was completed.

April. Gen. "Mad" Anthony Wayne, in charge of troops, descended the Ohio River to Cincinnati.

November 9. The first newspaper printed in Cincinnati, The Centinel of the Northwest Territory, appeared. It became the Freeman's Journal in 1796. It was run until November 1800 and then moved to Chillicothe.

1794   January 11. The first two riverboats from Cincinnati to Pittsburgh were announced in the Centinel of the Northwest Territory.

June 28. The Centinel announced that a postal communication was established between Pittsburgh and Cincinnati.

December 27. Nova Caesarea Harmony Lodge No. 2, Free Masonry, was formally established. The charter had been obtained from the Grand Lodge of New Jersey in 1791, but Dr. Burnet, who obtained it, was absent at the time.

1795   A new courthouse was constructed.

October 29. Griffin Yeatman announced the opening of an inn in the house recently occupied by Mr. Mathew Winton.

1797   May. William Henry Harrison was made captain and given command of Fort Washington.

1799   A mail route was established between Cincinnati and Chillicothe.

February 4. A meeting of the county representatives at Cincinnati led to the appointment of a group to create a state government.

Spring. The Western Spy and Gazette appeared. It became The Whig in 1809 and then The Advertiser. It survived until 1811.

May 1. Griffin Yeatman advertised that any family could use his water pump for twenty-five cents per week, to be paid each Monday morning.

September 10. Francis Menessier advertised in the Western Spy that he would teach French in the evenings Monday to Friday.

October. William McFarland began to make earthenware in Cincinnati. James and Robert Caldwell began the same work in February 1801.

1800   The population of Cincinnati was 2,540.

March. Robert Stubbs opened a classical school, the Newport Academy.

December 18. Dr. Daniel Drake came to Cincinnati at the age of fifteen.

1801   The Cincinnati Theatre opened.

November 26. The Territorial Assembly reassembled at Chillicothe. The territory was divided into three states by an act of Congress. Chillicothe was designated as the capitol of Ohio.

CHRONOLOGY

INCORPORATION OF THE CITY

1802   A brick courthouse was built. It burned down in 1814.

January 1. An act of the legislature incorporated the town of Cincinnati. It also changed the seat of the county government from Chillicothe to Cincinnati.

February 13. A group of citizens met at Yeatman's Tavern and decided to establish a library, which was opened March 6, 1802.

July 14. At a meeting in the new courthouse, a fire company was created.

1803   The Methodist Society was founded.

The First Bank was formed.

March 4. A meeting was held to form the Miami Exporting Company for trade. Its first directorate was elected on June 16. It was chartered by the first General Assembly of the new state of Ohio. It eventually became a bank.

March 29. After a destructive fire, an ordinance was passed establishing a night watch. Citizens, twenty-one and over, were arranged into classes of twelve each.

1804   The city began to regulate contagious diseases.

December 9. <u>The Liberty Hall and Cincinnati Mercury</u> was founded.

1805   October 10. Edward B. Hannegan's school was opened.

1806   The "Old Stone Church," a Methodist church, was erected.

The New Jerusalem, Swedenborgian, Church was founded.

1807   The city council authorized a committee of men to raise $6,000 by lottery for the benefit of the University of Cincinnati. It was never held.

March. The Miami Exporting Company opened a banking office.

May 1. Gambling was prohibited.

1808

Peter Williams contracted for carrying the mails between Louisville and Cincinnati; Cincinnati and Lexington; and Cincinnati and Greenville, Ohio.

The Circulating Library Society was started.

July. The Cincinnati Fire Bucket Company was organized. The company had a willow basket on a four-wheeled truck in which the fire buckets were placed.

1810

Washington Fire Company Number 1 was organized.

February 16. Captain John Kidd died. He bequeathed the rents of some of his land to be applied to the education of poor children and youth of Cincinnati.

July 11. Ordinances were passed regulating child delinquency and requiring the filling up of stagnant pools.

October. A public meeting was held to form another bank. The Farmers' and Mechanics' Bank received a charter for five years in 1812.

October 27. "The New Orleans" was the first steamboat to come to Cincinnati.

1813

The First Baptist Church was formed. The congregation split into two parts in 1816.

The Friends (Quakers) established themselves in the city.

The council authorized the purchase of a fire engine. It was procured in 1816.

The council passed an ordinance regulating weights and measures.

The School of Literature and Art was founded.

January 13. The first number of Liberty Hall was published.

May 10. An ordinance was passed requiring a physician to leave a memorandum of the reason for the death of a person.

1814   The council passed an ordinance regulating street lighting.

The Shell Bark Theatre opened.

The Miami Bible Society was formed to provide Bibles to the poor; Rev. O.M. Spencer was its first president.

The Bank of Cincinnati was opened for business, but it was not incorporated until 1816.

John H. Piatt and Company opened as the first private bank in the city.

The German Lutherans and Presbyterians joined forces to form the German Lutheran Congregation.

The <u>Spirit of the West</u> was first published. Only forty-four issues appeared.

June. The First District Medical Society, which had been authorized by the legislature on February 8, 1812, began to meet.

December 13. The <u>Liberty Hall</u> issued an invitation for a meeting of those interested in creating a hall for performances. The group eventually erected a small frame building on the site of the future Columbia Theatre.

December 26. O.M. Spencer, William Irwin, and Ethan Stone, presidents of the Miami Bank, the Farmers' and Mechanics' Bank, and the Bank of Cincinnati respectively, announced that they would discontinue the payment of notes in specie.

1815   William Carry was the first mayor of Cincinnati.

Daniel Drake published his <u>Statistical View, Or Picture of Cincinnati</u>, in order to encourage immigration to the city.

The first hospital was opened.

Cincinnati began its purification campaign to clear up the streams and swamps.

January 10. The Ohio General Assembly passed the Act of Incorporation of the Town of Cincinnati, repealing the act of 1802.

January 11. An announcement was made in the <u>Liberty Hall</u> of the formation of the thespian society.

February 4. The Lancastrian Society was founded by an act of the legislature. It was run by Edmund Harrison.

July 13. The <u>Cincinnati Gazette</u> was first published. It combined with the <u>Liberty Hall</u> on December 11.

1816

A fire engine was purchased by Gen. John S. Gano for the use of Relief Fire Company No. 2.

January 19. The Presbyterian Church of the Covenant was organized.

October 10. The Cincinnati Harmonical Society was founded.

1817

The First Episcopal Church was founded.

Jesse Reeder built a water tank using horses to run elevators that lifted the water, which he then sold to water carts.

The African Society, for spiritual and educational benefit of blacks, was formed.

The Sunday School Union Society was established.

January 27. The Cincinnati Bank of the United States, chartered by the United States in 1816, was established.

March 31. The Cincinnati Manufacturing Company was given the exclusive right of carrying water from the river by pipes to the houses and stores.

May 18. The Episcopal Christ Church was organized.

1818

The Cincinnati and Wesley Sunday Schools were established.

The Western Navigators' Bible and Tract Society was established to distribute religious literature among the sailors on the inland waters.

The Western Museum was established.

Elum P. Langdon established the Cincinnati Reading Room.

June. The <u>Western Spy</u> appeared as an enlarged sheet.

June 23. <u>The Inquisitor and Cincinnati Advertiser</u> appeared.

November 5. The Cincinnati banks suspended specie payments.

November 10. Dr. Daniel Drake delivered the first medical lecture to a few students beginning a project for a medical school. It was abandoned April 18, 1819.

1819

The third courthouse was completed. It burned down on July 9, 1849.

The Columbia Theatre, sometimes called the Globe, was built. It burned in 1834.

The Church of Walnut Hills was organized. The village was then separate from Cincinnati.

The Phoenix Foundry was established.

The Sunday School Society of the Episcopal Church was founded.

The Episcopal Singing Society was formed.

The Haydn Society was organized.

The first city directory appeared.

The Cincinnati Medical Society was formed. It expired in the same year.

The Humane Society was founded.

The first Catholic society was organized.

The first insurance company was instituted.

January. The Ohio General Assembly passed an act authorizing the incorporation of Cincinnati College.

January 9. <u>The Western Spy</u> became <u>The Western Spy and Cincinnati General Advertiser</u>.

January 19. The Medical College of Ohio was incorporated by the legislature with Dr. Daniel Drake at its head.

February 5. An act of the legislature made Cincinnati a city. The charter was in force until March 1, 1827. Isaac Burnet was mayor.

Fall. The first Jewish group met for worship in the county during the High Holy Days.

October 2. A fire ordinance was passed to put the department on a better basis.

November. Joseph Buchanan began to issue the weekly <u>Literary Cadet</u>. After twenty-three numbers it assumed the title <u>The Western Spy and Literary Cadet</u>.

November 5. Independent Fire Company Number 3 was organized. Shortly thereafter the Franklin Fire Engine and Hose Company was organized as Company Number 4.

1820

The population of Cincinnati was 9,642.

Protection Company Number 1 formed with the object of saving lives and property as well as to guard against robberies during fires.

Cincinnati College was formally organized with Elijah Slack as president.

January 3. The Medico-Chirurgical Society was founded with Daniel Drake as president. The last meeting was held in March, 1822.

March 8. A building dedicated to drama was opened on Second Street. The building was sold for taxes in 1825. It was destroyed by fire on April 4, 1834.

May. Fire Engine Company Number 4 began operations. It was called the Eagle Company Number 4 in 1826.

1821

The Apprentices' Library was founded.

Jas. Gilmore and Company was founded as a private bank. It was absorbed by the National Bank of Commerce in 1878.

Enon Baptist Church was formed. Its name was changed to the First Baptist Church of Cincinnati on March 5, 1838.

Christ Church, the first Catholic church, was built.

An act was passed providing for the care of the poor at the old Commercial Hospital as well as an expensive system of outdoor relief.

Olio was first published. The Times also appeared.

A charter amendment was passed providing that the clerk and treasurer be appointed by the council.

January 22. The Cincinnati Hospital was organized as the Commercial and Lunatic Asylum.

February 21. The Cincinnati Medical Association was founded; Robert Selman was president.

June 19. The See of Cincinnati was created by Papal Bull. Reverend Edward Fenwick was appointed the first bishop.

1822   The Society for Investigation was founded to solve profound problems of life.

The Young Men's Mercantile Library Association was formed.

March. Dr. John D. Godman issued the first number of the Western Quarterly Reporter.

July. An advertisement of the opening of the Pavilion Theatre appeared.

1823   Dr? Locke established the Cincinnati Female Academy.

1824   The city charter was amended.

The First District Medical Society of Ohio was instituted by Dr. John Rigers and others.

The Emporium was first issued. The National Crisis also first appeared. It soon was consolidated with the Emporium and the Independent Press.

The Dennison House, one of the oldest hotels in the state, was established.

January 1. The <u>Literary Gazette</u> was founded.

January 18. Bene Israel (Children of Israel) Congregation was established.

September 26. Thomas Hughes died, leaving his property to establish a school.

December 27. An act was passed dividing the city and township into four election districts corresponding to the four wards, as well as providing for the holding of elections.

1825   The Franklin Society was organized for scientific research.

Construction of the Ohio and the Miami Canals was authorized.

May. Peter Benson was sent from Philadelphia to establish another branch of the United States Bank.

May 18. The cornerstone of the Sycamore Street Cathedral was laid. It was dedicated December 17, 1826.

May 19. The Marquis de Lafayette visited Cincinnati.

1826   The <u>Ohio Medical Repository</u> was founded. It later reappeared as the <u>Western Medical and Physical Journal</u>.

William Woodward turned over some valuable land to the city to create the Woodward Free Grammar School. It was incorporated on January 24, 1827. Construction of the building was begun on October 31, 1831.

Frederick Eckstein inaugurated the New Academy of Fine Arts.

Benjamin Drake founded the Cincinnati <u>Chronicle</u>. It merged with the <u>Cincinnati Mirror</u> in 1834. It was renamed the <u>Chronicle</u> in 1839.

<u>Die Ohio Chronik,</u> a secular German paper, first appeared. It did not last long.

January. The Ohio Insurance Company was incorporated with T. Goodman as president.

August 25. The Western Tiller, an agricultural paper, was first issued. It lasted for one year.

December 17. The cornerstone of St. Peter's Cathedral was laid.

1827

January. The Cincinnati Equitable Company was incorporated.

January 26. The Second Act of Incorporation of Cincinnati was passed. The term of the mayor was increased to two years.

Isaac G. Burnet was reelected mayor.

May. The pamphlet Western Magazine and Review, edited by Timothy Flint, appeared.

June 25. The first number of the Daily Gazette was issued.

1828

St. Paul's Parish, Episcopal, was organized.

The First Congregational Church, Unitarian, was organized.

The Third Presbyterian Church was established.

Frank's Gallery of Fine Arts was founded.

The city council created subterranean sewers.

The city charter was amended during 1828-1829 to enable the city to undertake the work of public instruction.

October 25. The Ohio Mechanics' Institute was founded by Mrs. Thomas Emery. It was incorporated in 1829. The first exposition was held in Cincinnati in May 1838.

1829

The following daily newspapers were begun: the Commercial Advertiser and the Daily Commercial Advertiser.

The Franklin Typographical Society of Cincinnati was organized.

The Second Presbyterian Church erected a large building. Lyman Beecher delivered sermons there beginning in 1830.

Fire Company Number 5 was organized.

Isaac G. Burnet was reelected Mayor.

January 22. The Third Presbyterian Church was organized.

February. The Central Christian Church was established.

February 11. Lane Theological Seminary was incorporated. It was the gift of Elnathan Kemper. Dr. Lyman Beecher was eventually appointed its chief administrator.

February 12. An act was passed dividing the city into ten school districts, two for each ward, and providing that the city council support the public schools.

Fall. The state legislature chartered the Commerical Bank, which later became the Commercial National Bank.

1830

The Fourth Presbyterian Church was organized.

The Cincinnati Fire Association was formed to regulate the department, take care of the sick and disabled members and to arbitrate differences.

The American was first issued.

January 18. The assembly granted a charter to the Congregation of the Children of Israel, Reformed. The Mount Street Temple was dedicated in 1869.

January 21. The First Congregational Church of Cincinnati was incorporated.

February 22. The Cincinnati Independent Fire Engine and Hose Company, known as the Silk Stocking Company or Rovers, was organized.

February 23. The general assembly incorporated the Ohio Canal Company and the Steubenville Railway Company.

May 23. The Unitarians first gathered in their own house of worship.

October. The Lyceum was opened for public debate.

November 9. The Sixth Street Baptist Church was organized by members of the Enon Baptist Church. It was incorporated on February 6, 1832.

December 23. Ohio Lodge Number 1 of the Odd Fellows was organized in Cincinnati.

1831

The Catholic Telegraph was established by Rev. Edward Fenwick.

The Hebrew Beneficent Society was founded.

Elisha Hotchkiss was elected mayor for one term.

March. The Cincinnati Savings Institution was organized. It was incorporated at the winter session of the legislature.

March 4. The Cincinnati Medical Society, second of that name, was founded. It was incorporated in February, 1833, and closed in 1838.

March 29. The Fifth Presbyterian Church was organized.

July. The Academic Pioneer, the first educational journal, appeared.

July 22. The Baptist Weekly appeared.

October 17. Bishop Edward Fenwick opened a Literary Institute for the higher instruction of youth called the Athenaeum, which later became St. Xavier College.

October 24. The opening exercises of Woodward High School were held.

1832

The Third Street Theatre was built.

St. Peter's Evangelical Protestant Church was organized.

Hall's Western Monthly Magazine first appeared.

The Cincinnati and St. Louis Railroad was chartered.

August. The Fire Guards were organized. They were police who restrained the crowds at fires. They continued until December, 1854.

September 20. A cholera epidemic began, which lasted thirteen months.

September 26. Bishop Fenwick died. He was succeeded by Dr. John Baptist Purcell in 1833.

1833

Samuel W. Davies was elected mayor. He was reelected several times and died in office in 1843.

The Daily Herald was first published.

The College of Teachers was opened.

John C. Wright, Timothy Walker, and Edward King founded the Law School.

Lippincott's Amphitheatre was opened.

Rev. Lyman Beecher came to Cincinnati from Litchfield, Connecticut, as president of Lane Theological Seminary. He was the father of Harriet Beecher Stowe, who gathered much material for her later writings, including Uncle Tom's Cabin. His younger daughter Catherine founded a young ladies' school.

January 15. The Cincinnati Fire Engine and Hose Company was incorporated. It was called the Flat Iron or Checked Shirt Company.

January 25. A charter was granted for the Cincinnati Orphan Asylum. It was founded because of the cholera epidemic of 1832, which had left so many orphans. It was opened in June.

February. The Franklin Bank received its charter. It merged with the Citizens National Bank in 1906.

May. The Society of St. Vincent de Paul was organized. It was a charitable organization of Catholic laymen.

1834

The Lafayette Bank was formed. It became the National Lafayette Bank in 1879 and merged with the First National Bank in 1905.

The Cross and the Western Christian Advocate first appeared.

The Young Men's Bible Society was established as an auxiliary to the American Bible Society.

The Eclectic Academy of Music was formed.

Provisions were made for the examination of teachers in the city.

A special charter was granted to the Cincinnati Law Library, but nothing was done until 1846.

The "Inquisition," a literary organization, was formed.

The Medical and Law Schools of Cincinnati College were established.

February. The Lafayette Bank of Cincinnati and the Ohio Life Insurance and Trust Company were incorporated.

March. The Democratic Intelligencer appeared for a short time.

March 1. The third act of incorporation for Cincinnati was passed. It was maintained until the new state constitution of 1851, although it was amended frequently.

July 31. The German Society was formed.

October. The Exchange Bank and Savings Institution was opened by John Bates and Company.

October 7. The Weltburger appeared as a Whig paper. It later became Der Deutsche Franklin, supporting Martin Van Buren.

1835   Samuel W. Davies was reelected mayor.

The African Union Baptist Church was founded.

Dr. Daniel Drake was asked to return to the Medical College of Ohio. When he could not agree with his rival John Morehead, Drake founded the Medical Department of Cincinnati College.

Dr. Drake opened the Cincinnati Hospital, which lasted until 1839.

The Academy of Fine Arts was organized.

Charles Hammond began publication of Truth's Advocate, an anti-Jackson campaign paper.

April 10. J.F. Conover founded the Daily Whig.

April 18. The Young Men's Mercantile Library Association was organized.

May 6. E.S. and Frederick Thomas issued the Daily Evening Post for a short time.

June. The Western Messenger, a Unitarian journal, was first published.

1836

The following newspapers were first published: the Volksblast edited by Charles Reemlin; the Western World, the first penny paper published by William A. Harper; and the Harrison campaign paper, the People's Echo.

The following journals appeared: the Family Magazine, which was launched by Eli Taylor and which survived for six years, and W.D. Gallagher's Western Literary Journal and Monthly Review.

John Bates, owner of the Exchange Bank, built and opened a theater on Sycamore Street.

The Cincinnati, Columbus and Cleveland Railroad was chartered.

March 11. The Little Miami Railroad was chartered.

April. James G. Birney moved to Cincinnati, and shortly thereafter The Philanthropist appeared.

1837

Mayor Samuel W. Davies was reelected.

The following publications were first published: W.D. Gallagher's Hesperian, which lasted until 1838; The Daily Express; the Common School Advocate, an educational journal which lasted until 1841; the Universal Advocate; and the

Westlicher Merker, which later became Der Deutsche Im Wesen and finally Volksfreund.

April. The Fire Department Insurance Company was incorporated for the benefit of department firemen who were ill or injured.

July 3. The National Theatre was opened.

1838 The Superior Court of Cincinnati was created, existing until the adoption of the Ohio Constitution in 1851. The new Superior Court of Cincinnati was created April 7, 1854. The election of judges occurred for the first time in May, 1854.

October 18. The Cincinnati Academy of Fine Arts was organized.

July. The Educational Disseminator began its brief career.

1839 Samuel W. Davies was reelected Mayor.

The Jewish congregation Bene Yeshurun was formed.

June 25. The city took possession of the water works.

October 22. The Cincinnati Chamber of Commerce was organized. It merged with the Industrial Bureau in 1910.

December. The Chronicle was established as a daily paper.

1840 The First Congregational Church in Cincinnati was organized.

April 25. The Spirit of the Times was established as a penny paper. It soon became the Daily Times.

October 1. The Athenaeum was taken over by the Jesuits and changed its name to St. Xavier College.

1841 Mayor Samuel W. Davies was reelected.

The First English Evangelical Lutheran Church was formed.

The Ladies' Repository, a monthly magazine, was first published and continued in publication until 1846.

The city council gave James Conover a twenty-five year franchise for use of the city streets for gas.

Bishop Purcell laid the cornerstone of St. Peter's Cathedral. It was consecrated November, 1845.

January 8. The Daily Times was first published.

June 25. A race riot occurred. A mob attacked the home of Cornelius Burnett and his sons, who were arrested for attacking Constable Robert Black and a slaveholder whose slave was traced to Burnett's home.

September. A riot occurred as a result of trouble between the Irish and the blacks. Another riot occurred in October.

September 19. The first general meeting of Bene Yeshurun Congregation was held. It was incorporated on February 28, 1842. With the arrival of Dr. Isaac Wise on April 20, 1854, the congregation became the banner bearer of Reformed Judaism.

1842   Drs. Talliafero, Vattier, Strader and Marshal established a hospital, the Hotel for Invalids.

The Sisters of Charity took charge of the hospital and called it St. John's Hotel for Invalids.

A bank riot occurred as a result of the Bank of Cincinnati's closing its doors.

The Cincinnati Astronomical Society was founded. Ormsby Mitchell raised the necessary funds, and Nicholas Longworth donated the land.

The Seventh Street Congregational Church was formed.

The city council created a day watch.

Dr. Lemidas M. Lawson founded the Western Lancet, which combined with the Medical Observer and was then called the Lancet and Observer.

W.D. Gallagher and George S. Bennett issued the Message, which was consolidated with the Enquirer after one month.

1843

January 10. The Miami Exporting Company had to close. A mob gathered and went out of control.

February 20. The First English Lutheran Church of Cincinnati was organized.

May 4. The Wesleyan Female College was organized at a meeting of Methodist Ministers.

Henry F. Spencer was elected mayor. He served four terms until 1851.

Emil Klauprecht established the Fliegende Blaetter.

February. The Cincinnati Horticultural Society was formed.

June. The German Liedertafel was organized.

August. The People's Paper was issued. Soon afterwards it became the morning edition of the Evening Times.

October 2. The Cincinnati Commerical issued its first number. It soon combined with the Gazette on January 4, 1883.

1844

Dr. Lawson began his public monthly Journal of Health, which was intended for the people. It suspended publication after two years.

The Western Rambler appeared, but it survived for only a short period of time.

The Citizens' Bank was opened. It became the Union National Bank in 1881 and was merged with the Ohio Valley National Bank in 1887.

The Reformed Jewish Congregation of Benai-Jeshurun was organized.

February. The Central Presbyterian Church of Cincinnati was organized. It was officially accepted by the Presbytery of Cincinnati on April 23, 1844.

August. The Cincinnati Historical Society was organized with James H. Perkins as the first president.

November. The <u>Western Literary Journal and Monthly Magazine</u> was first published. It ceased publication in April, 1845.

1845

Joseph Herron opened Herron's Seminary, a private school for boys and young men. It lasted eighteen years until Herron's death in 1863.

The Jewish Hospital was organized.

The State Bank of Ohio was created.

February. The Colored Orphan Asylum of Cincinnati was chartered. It had been established in 1844.

March 10. A charter was granted to the Eclectic Medical Institute.

May. The Queen City Hook and Ladder Company entered the fire department.

August 28. The rural Spring Grove Cemetary was dedicated.

1846

Stephen Foster came to Cincinnati and worked for his brother for three years until he returned to Pittsburgh in 1849. It was at this time that he gained additional background that enabled him to write for black minstrel shows.

The Cincinnati to Springfield Railroad was completed. It was the first in Cincinnati. The Sandusky branch was completed in 1848, and the connection was made with Columbia at Xenia.

A number of German Polish Jews united to establish the Adath Israel Congregation.

The Walnut Street Baptist Church was established.

The Gesang-und Bildungs-verein Deutscher Arbeiter was established. It was the first German organization with female voices. It was disbanded in 1852.

Arrangements were made to employ private watchmen for the merchants. They were to be compensated by the merchants but were to have the same powers as the other city watchmen.

The Cincinnati Library and the New England Society were organized.

October. The School Friend was launched by the school book publisher W.B. Smith and Company. Early in 1850 The Ohio School Journal merged with this publication. It ceased publication in September, 1851.

1847

The Western Art Union was established.

January. Lucius Hine began publication of the Herald of Truth.

April 22. Levi Coffin came to Cincinnati. He soon launched an antislavery campaign and became a leader in the Underground Railroad.

June 5. The Cincinnati Law Library Association was incorporated.

1848

The Cincinnati Relief Union was organized as a society for the relief of the worthy poor.

The Eintracht, a society of Germans, was founded. It lasted one year.

The Swiss musicians were organized as the Schweizer-Verein.

The Medico-Chirurgical Society, the second of that name, was organized.

Construction of the Cincinnati, Hamilton and Dayton Railroad was begun. It opened in 1851.

The Great West was first issued. It merged with the Weekly Columbian and was called the Columbian and Great West.

February. The Eighth Presbyterian Church was organized. It was dissolved in 1862.

February 18. The Jewish Congregation of Ahabeth Achim, the Society of Brotherly Love, was founded.

An act was passed providing that the special road district of Millcreek Township be annexed to the city.

August 28. The Spring Grove Cemetary was consecrated.

October 8. The teachers of the First Mission Sunday School of the Central Christian Church met to form the Young Men's Society of Inquiry. The title of the organization was changed to the Cincinnati Society of Religious Inquiry and Young Men's Christian Union in 1853. Then, in 1858, it became known as the Young Men's Christian Union, and finally Young Men's Christian Association in 1863.

1849

The Jewish Hospital Association was founded.

The first Saengerbund Festival was held.

February 15. The Gibson House (a hotel) was opened.

April 13. The Talmud Yelodin Institute was opened. English as well as Hebrew and German subjects were taught. It was chartered in 1851.

October 29. The Literary Club was started.

November 5. Dr. Daniel Drake was recalled to the Medical College. He died on November 6, 1852.

1850

The population of Cincinnati was 115,435.

The <u>Western Magazine</u> began publication.

The Burnet House was formally opened with a grand ball and housewarming.

The First German Presbyterian Church was organized.

March 22. An act was passed adding the Town of Fulton to the city and township of Cincinnati. The annexation was approved in a vote of the residents in October, 1854. It became the seventeenth ward in January, 1855.

July 19. Cincinnati was raised to the rank of archdiocese, and Bishop Purcell was created archbishop. He resigned after the development of serious financial chaos in 1879. His successor, William Henry Elder, was made coadjutor in January 1880. He succeeded to the archbishopric after the death of Purcell on July 4, 1883.

October 7. The House of Refuge was formally opened.

1851 The Ohio State Constitution was amended, providing for the general incorporation of all cities in the state.

Drs. B. Ehrman, Adam Miller, and G.W. Bigler established the Cincinnati Journal of Homeopathy.

The American Psychological Journal was begun by Dr. Mead.

Mark P. Taylor was elected mayor.

The Germans rioted because of the presence of the Papal Nuncio Bedini. They were ill-disposed toward anyone who would suppress their liberties in their homeland and thought that Bedini was such a person.

The fourth courthouse was built and served in that capacity until March 29, 1884.

March 7. A charter was granted for the Cincinnati College of Medicine and Surgery.

September. The Cincinnati Medical Library Association was founded. It was opened with Dr. Drake's first lecture on January 9, 1852.

November 18. The Cincinnati Medical Society, third of that name, was organized.

1852 Joseph H. Pulte and H.P. Gatchell undertook the publication of the American Magazine of Homeopathy and Hydropathy.

Miami Medical College was opened. The first faculty meeting was held July 22, 1852. Strife soon occurred and many faculty members joined the Medical College of Ohio. A faculty was organized to revive the College in 1865.

The City Infirmary was opened.

November. The Western Tract Society was established as the American Reform Tract and Book Society.

1853 The first Grand Opera House was built. It burned down in January, 1901. A new one was built on the site of the old.

David T. Snellbaker was elected mayor.

Pen and Pencil, a weekly magazine, was begun.

The Genius of the West first appeared. It lasted until July, 1856.

The Young Men's Gymnastic Association was opened.

Benn Pittman established the Phonographic Institute. By 1904 the Phonographic Amanuensis was the leading textbook of the Benn Pittman system.

Summer. A sunday school was established on Mt. Auburn. Out of this grew the Mt. Auburn Baptist Church, established in 1856.

July. The Parlor Magazine appeared with Alice Cary on the staff for a period of time. It eventually merged with The West American Review. The last two numbers were issued under the title West American Monthly.

November. The Cumminsville Presbyterian Church building was dedicated. It was admitted to the Presbytery in 1855.

December. The Spencer House (a hotel) was opened.

1854   Mrs. Sarah Worthington King Peter helped to found an Academy of Fine Arts.

1855   A large branch of the Brotherhood of Locomotive Engineers was organized in Cincinnati.

James J. Faran was elected mayor.

The Lick Run Cemetary was established by the Sh'erith Israel Congregation.

Fallis and Company was founded. It became the Merchants' National Bank in 1865 and then merged with the First National Bank in 1909.

Abraham Lincoln and Edwin M. Stanton met each other in Cincinnati. They were retained in the lawsuit of McCormick vs. Mormy.

E. Kinney and Company, a banking house, was founded. It failed in 1877. George H. Bussing and Company formed the Walnut Street Bank, which also failed in 1877.

The Public Library was organized.

April. The Know-Nothing riots occurred when foreign elements came into collision with the party that wanted America for the Americans.

Summer. Philip W. Bickel was engaged as a Baptist missionary to work among the Germans. Subsequently the converts reorganized and were recognized as an independent church.

July 26. The Episcopal Church of the Advent was organized in Walnut Hills.

September 3. The Congregation Sh'erith Israel was organized in Gerson's Hotel. It dedicated its new synagogue in September 1860.

1856.   The German-American Cecilia Society was formed.

The Poplar Street Church was formed beginning with a sunday school. The church was formally organized in January, 1859.

January 5. The Episcopal Calvary Church in Clifton was organized.

May. The Phoenix Club was organized as a German organization of Jewish men.

July. The Ohio School Library was organized by arrangement with the Ohio Mechanics' Institute.

November. The Associate Reformed Church was founded in the Engine House Hall.

November 23. The Pioneer Association was first opened.

1857   The Ohio and Mississippi Railroad was completed.

Nicholas W. Thomas was elected mayor.

January 14. The city council passed an ordinance regulating

the management of the City Infirmary, Commercial Hospital, Pesthouse, City Burying Ground, and granting of outdoor relief to the poor.

February 26. A branch of the Order of the Sisters of the Good Shepherd was established in Cincinnati.

March 5. The Academy of Medicine of Cincinnati was organized.

June 27. The Mannerchor of Cincinnati was organized, uniting the following music societies: the Liedertafel, Saengerbund, and Germanic Society.

1858

Dr. A.H. Baker began publication of the monthly <u>Cincinnati Medical News</u>. After the second year it was called the <u>Cincinnati Medical and Surgical News</u>. It was suspended in 1863.

The Sisters of Mercy came to Cincinnati from the Mother House of Mercy in Dublin, Ireland. They were brought over by Mrs. Sarah Worthington King Peter of Cincinnati.

Joseph F. Larki and Company, a banking house, was established in 1858. It became the Metropolitan National Bank in 1881 and finally failed in 1888.

The Bank of the Ohio Valley was founded.

C.F. Adae and Company, the German Savings Institution, was founded. It failed in 1878.

The grounds of the former Presbyterian Cemetary, which had been removed, were purchased and developed into Washington Park.

September. St. Mary's Hospital was given its building. It was founded by the Sister of the Poor of St. Francis.

1859

The first purchase of land for Eden Park was made from J.S.G. Burt for $14,000. The last purchase was made in 1893. The total cost was $1,693,427.81.

Richard M. Bishop was elected mayor.

The Longview Asylum was formed. It had been part of the Commercial Hospital.

March 14. The legislature passed an act constituting a board of police commissioners. Four men were to be appointed by the mayor, the police judge and the city auditor. The four appointed, and the mayor, were to form the board of commissioners.

April. General Winfield Scott was a guest of the city.

Jenny Lind sang in the city.

May. The publication of The Ohio Teacher began.

July 13. Six routes for a system of street railroads were laid out.

September 14. The first car on a street railroad line was run. It was a horse-car system.

1860   The Dial was founded and issued throughout the year.

January. The Journal of Progress in Education, School and Political Economy and the Useful Arts appeared and continued until August, 1861.

January 10. The Protestant Home of the Friendless and Foundlings was inaugurated.

July 25. The seventh streetcar route was established in Cincinnati on Front Street.

September 29. The Prince of Wales arrived.

1861   The Grand Opera House was opened.

February 12. President-elect Abraham Lincoln passed through Cincinnati on the way to Washington and was given a great reception.

April 1. George Hatch was elected mayor. He was the representative of the extreme sentiment of deference and concession to the South.

April 5. The authorities permitted some cannon assigned from Baltimore to Jackson, Mississippi, for the use of the Southern Confederacy, to pass through the city.

April 15. The first great meeting for endorsing the Union and prosecuting the war was held at the Catholic Institute.

April 17. The citizens received news of the assault on Fort Sumter and the beginning of hostilities.

Rutherford B. Hayes presided at a special meeting of the Cincinnati Literary Club. A committee of three was appointed to consider the formation of a military company. Thirty-three of the men present began to drill, forming the Burnet Rifles.

1862

The United Jewish Cemetary was consecrated.

The private banking firm of Hewson, White and Company was formed. Its deposits were transferred to the Fourth National Bank in 1875.

Espy Heidelbach and Company was founded. It became the Ohio Valley National Bank in 1886. It merged with the First National Bank in 1905.

1863

The Harmonic Society of Cincinnati was formed.

The Yale Club was organized. It was said to be the oldest alumni society in America.

Leonard Harris was elected mayor.

July. John Morgan of the Confederacy threatened Cincinnati. He was eventually captured and imprisoned in the Ohio Penitentiary from which he escaped on November 27.

August. The First National Bank of Cincinnati was opened under the National Bank Act of February 20, 1863. During the latter part of the year the Second, Third, and Fourth National Banks were established.

1864

The American Homeopathist first appeard. It merged with the Ohio Medical and Surgical Reporter in 1868.

Lieutenant Samuel B. Davis of the Confederacy was tried at Cincinnati. He was found guilty, although he had destroyed the evidence and gave an eloquent defense. He was sentenced to be hung, but President Lincoln commuted the sentence to imprisonment in Fort Warren where Davis remained until the end of the war.

CHRONOLOGY

1865

The Children's Home was organized under the leadership of Murray Shipley.

A law was passed giving the city council authority to procure the necessary funds for a police alarm system. It was installed by J.F. Kennard and Company of Boston in 1866.

Mayor Leonard A. Harris was reelected.

The city council organized the board of health.

The St. Nicholas Hotel was opened.

The Central National Bank was established.

The Ohio National Bank was founded. It was merged with the First National Bank in 1905.

The Parish of the Episcopal Christ Church, Glendale, was founded.

March 4. The Cincinnati Masonic Library Association was organized.

May 12. The cornerstone for the Plum Street Jewish Temple was laid.

November. Wood's Theatre was built on the site of the People's Theatre on the southeast corner of Sixth and Vine.

POST CIVIL WAR CINCINNATI

1866

The Associated Artists group was formed.

Louis H. Hopkins presented the city with one acre on Mount Auburn for a park.

Drs. George C. Blackman and Theophilus Parvin of the Medical College of Ohio began a monthly, The Cincinnati Journal of Medicine. It became the Western Journal of Medicine, which was published in Indianapolis in 1870. It was absorbed by the Lancet and Observer in 1875.

The Second German Presbyterian Church was organized.

February 25. The Episcopal Grace Church in College Hill was organized.

1867

March 20. A meeting was held of bankers at the Lafayette Bank to form a clearing house, which was formally established on April 14.

Joseph A. Hamann and Company, a banking house, was established.

Charles F. Wilstach was elected mayor.

Andrews Bissell and Company, a banking house, was founded.

The Cincinnati Savings Society was organized.

The Cincinnati Conservatory of Music was established by Miss Clara Baur.

Dr. John Draper organized a baseball team, the Cincinnati Juniors.

The Red Stocking Baseball Team was organized. It toured the country in 1869.

Grace Church in Avondale was organized.

January 20. A bridge was opened over the Ohio River at Covington. It was built with Cincinnati capital.

August. The Merchants' National Bank absorbed the Ohio National Bank.

September. The Ohio Federation of the National Association of Baseball Clubs was organized by Aaron G. Champion. Fourteen clubs were represented at the convention.

1868

The New York Clipper offered nine gold medals to the baseball players attaining the best averages. Harry Wright, Fred Waterman, and J. William Johnson of Cincinnati earned three.

The Cincinnati Gallery of Fine Arts was organized.

The Young Women's Christian Association of Cincinnati was founded.

The National Normal, an education journal, first appeared.

The Protectory for Boys was founded to offer neglected boys a home and an education to become good Catholics.

A meeting at the law offices of Tilden, Sherman and Moulton was held to make arrangements to make the Cincinnati baseball team a professional one. It was the first regular professional team in the country, formally organized in 1869.

The Miami Valley Savings Society was established.

Dr. J.A. Thacker founded <u>The Cincinnati Medical Repertory</u>. In 1872 its name was changed to the <u>Medical News</u>. It was suspended in 1890.

April 21. The Avondale Presbyterian Church was organized.

1869

John F. Torrence was elected mayor.

The Harvard Club was organized by the alumni living in Cincinnati.

The Kehilah Kedosha Beth Tefilla, House of Prayer, Jewish Congregation was founded.

January 1. Instruction began at Cincinnati University.

January 4. The McMiken School of Design was opened. It was founded through a bequest to Cincinnati by Charles McMiken, who had died in 1858. Its administration was transferred from the University of Cincinnati to the Cincinnati Museum Association in 1884.

April 28. The Senate passed a bill to construct a railroad. The House passed the same a week later, May 4. Cincinnati then voted to raise $10 million in bonds to construct the Cincinnati and Southern Railway.

May 31. The Red Stocking Baseball Team started on a nationwide tour. It returned on July 1.

September. Storrs Township was annexed as the Twenty-first Ward. Walnut Hills, Mount Auburn, and Clintonville were added as the Twenty-second and Twenty-third Wards.

August. The first Cincinnati Industrial Exposition was held.

November. Camp Washington and Lick Run were annexed.

November 12. A great part of Spencer Township was added.

1870

The Red Stockings Baseball Club was broken up. The National League was formed in 1876. Cincinnati was a member of it for five years. Then the Reds joined the American Association until 1889. It then rejoined the National League in 1890 and has been a member of the League since then.

Seasongood, Netter Company was formed. It became the Equitable National Bank and then merged with the Merchants National Bank in 1905.

The <u>Public School Journal</u> was first published.

January 19. The Cincinnati Society of Natural History was organized. It was incorporated in June.

March 1. The legislature permitted the trustees of Cincinnati Hospital to admit medical students, not pupils of the Medical College of Ohio, to witness medical and surgical treatment of patients.

September 16. The Cincinnati Hospital Medical Library was established by the Cincinnati Hospital in conjunction with the Cincinnati Public Library. The hospital library was withdrawn from the public library on January 29, 1874.

1870

The population of Cincinnati was 216,329.

September 21. An industrial exposition was opened, which inaugurated a series of movements in American between 1871 and 1875.

October. The Carlisle House was opened.

November 1. The United States government established a weather bureau station in Cincinnati.

December 9. The <u>Israelite</u> announced that Mr. Henry Adler of Laurenceburg had offered a sum of money to the Cincinnati Congregation Bene Yeshurun under Dr. Wise for the establishment of a college to train rabbis.

1871

S.S. Davis was elected mayor.

The faculty of the Medical College of Ohio began publication of <u>The Clinic,</u> a weekly journal. It was merged with the <u>Lancet and Observer</u> in 1878 and became known as the <u>Lancet and Clinic.</u> In 1886 it was called the <u>Lancet-Clinic.</u>

The Ohio State Society for the Protection of Game and Fish was formed. It changed its name to the Cuvier Club in 1875.

The Town of Columbia was added to the First Ward.

July 12. St. Philip's Episcopal Church was formed.

October 16. A fountain, presented by Henry Probasco as a memorial for his brother-in-law, Mr. Tyler Davidson, was unveiled.

1872   The <u>Star</u> was founded.

January 24. The Cincinnati Bar Association was formed.

Summer. At the proposal of some leading citizens, a committee was appointed with George Ward Nichols presiding. It organized a festival that was held in the Saengerbund building in 1873.

August 15. The Walnut Street Baptist Church was organized.

Fall. The Pulte Medical College was opened for homeopathy.

1873   Cumminsville and Woodburn were annexed to the city.

The following banking institutions were organized: the German-American Bank of Hakman, Hengehold and Company; the First German Loan Association formed by Herman Levi and Company; and the German Banking Company, which later became the German National Bank in 1881.

George W.C. Johnston was elected mayor.

The legislature changed the police board. Four men were to be chosen at the spring election.

Dr. Wilson published the <u>Cincinnati Medical Advance.</u> The journal was moved to Ann Arbor, Michigan in 1886.

St. Joseph's Maternity Hospital and Infant Asylum was founded.

The Society for the Preservation of Cruelty to Animals and for the Protection of Children was formed. It was incorporated in 1875 and reincorporated in 1878.

The Zoological Society of Cincinnati was founded.

August 25. The new Board of Fire Commissioners was appointed by the mayor and confirmed by the council. It had been created by the legislature.

October. Burnet Woods, consisting of 63.5 acres, was leased as a park. It was purchased in 1881 at the cost of $746,855.68.

1874 The mayor, George Johnston, took charge of police affairs. He did away with the Board of Police Commissioners.

The Queen City Optimists' Club was founded.

March. The Expressman's Aid Society was established.

March 17. The Massey Medical and Scientific Library was founded with a gift of Dr. W.H. Massey of his medical and scientific works to the public library.

September 14. The Grand Hotel was opened. It was owned and operated by a stock company with Theodore Cook as president.

October. The City Club was organized, which was chiefly social in its aim.

Fall. St. Luke's Episcopal Church was organized.

1875 William S. Grosbeck donated $50,000 for band concerts in Burnet Woods on Saturday afternoons throughout the summer.

Mayor George W.C. Johnston was reelected.

Andrews Bissell and Company was organized as a National Bank.

The Western German Bank was formed.

May. Reuben R. Springer offered to give $125,000 for a music hall if an equal sum should be raised by the citizens.

The hall cost much more, and Mr. Springer eventually contributed $235,000.

September 18. The zoological garden was opened. It had been organized in 1873.

October 3. The Hebrew Union College was opened under the leadership of Dr. Isaac M. Wise. On July 11, 1883, four members of the senior class received rabbinical degrees.

1876

Joseph Longworth presented the art department of the University of Cincinnati with $59,000 on condition that it would add $10,000 for the construction of an art academy. His son, the Hon. Nicholas Longworth, donated $371,631 to the institution, after which the name was changed to the Art School of Cincinnati.

The Republican convention was held in the city. Rutherford B. Hayes was nominated for president, and he was elected in November.

The Obstetrical Society of Cincinnati was organized.

The Police Relief Association was established for the aid of sick or disabled policemen and families.

S. Kuhn and Sons, a banking firm, was established. It was absorbed by the Fifth-Third National Bank in 1909.

January. The National Bank of Commerce was opened with a capital stock of $300,000.

April 19. St. Thomas Parish, Episcopal, was organized.

December 26. The benevolent and Protective Order of Elks Lodge was first opened. It was chartered on December 11, 1877 and incorporated January 18, 1889.

1877

The legislature reestablished the Cincinnati Board of Police Commissioners.

The Bank of Cincinnati was formed. It was absorbed by the Citizens' National Bank in 1881.

The Queen City Bank was opened.

R.M. Moore was elected mayor.

January 18. The Women's Centennial Executive Committee of Cincinnati met and resolved to reorganize as an association to advance women's work in art. The society met on April 28 to complete the work of the Art Museum.

1878

The Bureaus of Medical Relief, Sanitary Inspection, Markets and Vital Statistics were created as a part of the board of health.

Dr. E.B. Stevens founded <u>The Obstetric Gazette</u>. It was discontinued in 1890.

The Hotel Emory was opened.

1879

Miss M. Louise McLaughlin organized the Pottery Club.

C. Jacob, Jr. was elected mayor.

The Associated Charities of Cincinnati was organized through the efforts of the Woman's Christian Association. Mrs. Sarah W. Bullock donated a building for the organization in 1894.

The Ohio Hospital for Women and Children was started with a free homeopathic dispensary.

John King donated his library of 2500 volumes to the public.

April. The Lafayette Bank and the National Bank of Commerce merged as the National Lafayette and Bank of Commerce.

July 23. The first train ran on the Southern Railroad.

October. The Clifton Presbyterian Church was begun with the establishment of a sunday school. It was developed into a Presbyterian mission on March 15, 1881.

December 13. The first meeting of women to establish a kindergarten association was held. It adopted its constitution on December 19 with Mrs. Alphonso Taft, mother of the future President William Howard Taft, as president.

1880

George B. Cox, future "Boss of Cincinnati," began his political activity.

The first train to Chattanooga, Tennessee, ran on the Cincinnati Southern Railroad.

A company was formed to light the city with electricity.

The Little Miami Depot was built.

The following banks were established: the Metropolitan National Bank, the Union National Bank; and the Exchange National Bank, which was absorbed by the Cincinnati National Bank in 1884.

The Security Insurance Company was formed.

The "Boy Preacher" Harrison held revival meetings and claimed 3,000 converts.

The Commercial Club was organized.

The Cincinnati Post was founded.

The Duckworth Democratic Club was organized.

A sharp contest occurred in the Republican municipal convention for the post of city treasurer. There were rumors that money had been dishonestly spent.

Mrs. Maria Longworth Storer opened the Rookwood Pottery.

June. The Times and Star newspapers were consolidated.

September. An exposition was opened at which it was announced that Charles W. West would give $150,000 for an art museum on the condition that an equal amount should be raised within a year.

November. The Citizens' National Bank was organized.

1881   William Means was elected mayor.

The Cincinnati Museum Association was incorporated.

April. The German Protestant Home for Aged Men was opened.

June. The German Banking Company was formed into the German National Bank.

November 9. The Bodman Widows' Home, a Protestant organization, was founded by Mrs. Lauretta Bodman Gibson.

1882   The Jewish Congregation Ohave Sholem was founded at the old Spencer House.

The Queen City National Bank was formed. It became the Fifth National Bank in 1888 and the Fifth-Third National Bank in 1908.

The Palace Hotel was opened.

A violent struggle occurred between the stricter and lower elements over the Sunday closing law.

The National Forestry Congress held its annual Meeting in Cincinnati.

The American Library Association held its annual meeting in the city.

January 7. The Parish of the Episcopal Church of the Epiphany was organized.

February 3. The council passed an ordinance permitting the erection of the art museum building in Eden Park.

Fall. The Cincinnati Reds won the American Association pennant.

1883   T.J. Stephens was elected mayor.

The Fidelity Safe Deposit and Trust Company and the Central Trust and Safe Deposit Company were organized.

The Cincinnati College of Medicine and Surgery admitted female students. In 1886 a separate department for women was established under the name of the Women's Medical College of Cincinnati. It continued as a separate department until 1890.

The Westminster Presbyterian Church was organized.

Heuck's Opera House was built.

The Commercial absorbed the Gazette.

February 15. The Ohio River rose to a level of 66 feet 4 inches, which was the greatest flood to that time.

May 18. The Jewish Home for the Aged and Infirm was founded.

1884   The Cincinnati National Bank absorbed the Exchange National Bank.

March 14. The United States Marine Hospital of Cincinnati was opened.

March 28. A riot occurred because of a protest over a lighter verdict of a jury for a white man, William Berner, than for a mulatto, Joseph Palmer. Both had murdered their employer William Kirk. The groups were incited at a meeting which was intended to be peaceful but got out of hand. The mob attacked and burned the jail and the courthouse. The militia had to be called in to restore order.

June 6. The Young Men's Blaine Club, a Republican organization, was formed on the day James G. Blaine was nominated for the presidency of the United States.

1885   Drs. A.B. Thrasher and F.W. Sage began publication of The Cincinnati Medical and Dental Journal. The dental feature was dropped in 1888, and The Cincinnati Medical Journal continued to be published until 1896.

The Alumni Association of Cincinnati College of Medicine and Surgery, which had been founded in 1851, began publication of the Cincinnati Medical Journal.

The Boys' Home of Cincinnati was founded and later incorporated in 1895 to protect, educate, and shelter newsboys, working boys, and homelss boys in general.

Amor Smith, Jr., a Republican, who ran on a reform platform, was elected mayor.

1886   Several serious railroad labor riots occurred.

The Fidelity National Bank was organized.

The Salvage Corps was organized by Henry F. Newman, a former fireman.

A group of citizens, mainly German, founded the <u>Bund fur Freiheit und Recht</u> to protest against agitation for a Sunday "blue law."

The Taxpayers' Association was founded. It eventually became involved in the reform movement in the city.

May 17. The art museum building in Eden Park was dedicated.

August. The Jewish Orthodox Congregation Beth Hamedrash Hagodol was founded.

December. The Ohio Valley National Bank was formed by the firm of Espy Heidelbach and Company. It merged with the Union National Bank in 1887.

1887

The Merchants and Manufacturers Association of Cincinnati was organized. It was incorporated in 1893.

The Jewish Shelter Home was founded.

The following banks were organized: the Atlas National Bank and the Market National Bank, as well as the City Hall Bank.

March 3. Three hundred Democratic businessmen banded together to nominate candidates for city office instead of through the primaries in order to avoid the influence of the Cox group.

April. The Calvary Presbyteran Church in Linwood was organized.

May. Seasongood Sons and Company organized the Equitable National Bank.

June. The Fidelity National Bank failed.

November. George B. Cox was successful as Governor Joseph B. Foraker's campaign manager for reelection in Hamilton County. Cox was then appointed state oil inspector.

1888

The Cincinnati Women's Press Club was founded. It became federated in 1890.

The Salvation Army was organized.

The zoological garden and its vicinity was annexed.

A bitter contest occurred over the Owen Law, which closed the saloons on Sunday.

February 22. The West End Republican Club was organized.

June 14. The German Deaconess Home and Hospital was founded.

July 4. The centennial anniversary of the founding of the city was celebrated.

November. George Cox was defeated in the election for county court clerk by John B. Peaslee.

November 5. The Stamina Republican League was founded.

December 27. The St. Francis Hospital began its work under the charter of the Sisters of St. Francis.

1889

The Cincinnati Training School for nurses opened. It was the first one west of the Alleghenies. Miss Annie Murray was the superintendent.

The Central Labor Council was founded. It published a monthly journal, The Chronicle.

February. The Committee of Five Hundred took the lead in the movement to enforce the Sunday laws.

Fall. Drs. Mary Elizabeth Osborn and Juliet Monroe Thorpe established a free dispensary for women and children. The foundation of the Presbyterian Hospital and the Laura Memorial Women's Medical College was chartered in 1890.

November. John Mosby, a Republican, and the candidate of George Cox and others, was elected mayor.

December 12. The Cincinnati Club was founded. It was incorporated in May 1890 for social and literary purposes.

1890

The Home for the Incurables was opened.

April. The legislature established a Free Public Employment Office.

May. The Union Savings Bank and Trust Company was organized.

May 1. The Presbyterian Hospital was organized.

October 1. The Women's State Hospital Medical College was opened.

1891

The Hotel Alms was constructed and opened.

The Opthalmic Hospital was founded by Dr. Robert Shattler.

The Gemilath Chesed Society was founded to aid Jewish immigrants attain self-help.

January. The Jewish Hospital School for Nurses was opened.

November. Mayor John Mosby was reelected.

1892

The Business Men's Club was formed. It was reincorporated in 1896 as the Young Men's Business Club to promote the best interests of Cincinnati.

1893

George Cox was successful in getting an ordinance passed permitting General Hickenlooper's Gas Company to enter the electric light field.

The Cincinnati Chapter of the Daughters of the American Revolution was established with Mrs. Brent Arnold as regent.

Avondale, Riverside, Clifton, Linwood, and Westwood were added to Cincinnati.

April 3. The Church of the Nativity was incorporated.

June. The New Christ Hospital was formally opened.

October 17. The Night Law School was opened.

October 21. The Cincinnati Chapter of the Daughters of the American Revolution was formally chartered.

November. The Protestant Episcopal Hospital for children was incorporated.

CHRONOLOGY 45

1894   The Cincinnati Woman's Club was organized with Miss Annie Laws as president.

The Tribune was started. It was consolidated with the Commercial Gazette in 1897 as the Commercial Tribune.

The Congregation Anshe Poland, Jewish, was organized.

June 10. St. Andrew's Episcopal Mission was begun.

November. J.A. Caldwell was elected mayor.

1896   The Brighton German Bank was opened.

The German Deaconess Home was opened.

The state legislature enacted the Rogers Law, which authorized the city to grant a fifty-year traction franchise. The fare was to be five cents and was subject to revision after twenty years and then every fifteen years thereafter.

The Bethesda Hospital was organized.

April 14. The United Jewish Charities of Cincinnati was established.

April 24. An act of the legislature was passed authorizing the governor of Ohio to appoint a commission to develop a water supply system for Cincinnati. This was to be the new water works.

1897   William Howard Taft was dean of the law school. He soon left to go into politics and government.

January 28. The Cincinnati Research Society was organized.

May 1. The Young Women's Improvement Club was organized under the Cincinnati Section of the Council of Jewish Women. Its aim was to raise girls out of the sphere of the factory.

November. Gustav Tafel was elected mayor.

1898   January 18. Braggs' Subdivision and Rose Hill were brought into Cincinnati.

September 5-11. The eleventh annual encampment of the Grand Army of the Republic was held in Cincinnati.

1899   November. Julius Fleischmann was elected mayor. This municipal election brought George Cox out into the open as a political boss. His candidate defeated the fusionist candidate Alfred Cohen.

THE TWENTIETH CENTURY

1900   The Population of Cincinnati was 325,902.

The Unity Bank and Savings Company was opened.

February. The Provident Savings and Trust Company was organized.

December. The Cincinnati Trust Company was formed. It was absorbed by the Provident Savings and Trust Company in 1911.

1901   April. Julius Fleischmann was reelected mayor.

1902   The Longsworth Act was passed by the state legislature in an attempt to make the governments of all cities in Ohio uniform.

Andrew Carnegie offered the city $180,000 for the building of six branch libraries.

The Columbia Bank and Savings Company was opened.

The Police Department was placed under the civil service rules.

December. Portions of Dehi Township were added to Cincinnati.

1903   The police department was placed under the charge of the Board of Public Safety, which was appointed by the mayor.

The Cosmopolitan Bank and Savings Company was opened.

The Home Savings Bank Company was founded.

The Southern Ohio Savings Bank was established, as well as the Security Savings Bank and Safe Deposit Company.

CHRONOLOGY 47

April. Mayor Julius Fleischman was reelected.

April 27. Henry Moeller was made coadjutor to Archbishop Elder with the right of succession. Rev. Elder died October 31, 1904.

May. The Clovernook Home for the Blind was opened. Mr. Proctor bought it and turned it over to the Trader sisters.

October. One hundred and sixty acres lying between Avondale and Bond Hill were annexed by Cincinnati. The city also added Winston Place, Evanston, Bond Hill, and Hyde Park during 1903.

1904   March 17. A portion of Milcreek Township was added to Cincinnati.

1905   Julius Fleischman was reelected mayor, defeating the fusionist candidate M.E. Ingalls.

The Hotel Lackman, the first fireproof hotel in the city, was opened.

November. Edward J. Dempsey, Democrat and fusion candidate, was elected governor of Ohio.

George Cox retired from politics.

1906   The City Club was formed to reform the evils of the municipal government.

The Hotel Havlin was opened.

The Parks Commission was appointed and $15,000 appropriated by the council to develop the park system. George E. Kessler of Kansas City was employed to map out the system of parks and boulevards.

May. The Ahabeth Achin - Sh'rith Israel Congregation was consolidated.

A trial of men, including George Cox, was held. They were accused of having taken money from the city treasury. Cox was indicted for perjury when the testimony of the others implicating him was accepted. The court ruled that taking the money under the circumstances was not a criminal act.

November 12. The Lyric Theatre was opened.

1907   The American National Bank was formed. It merged with the Fifth-Third National Bank in 1908.

The Cincinnati Anti-Tuberculosis League was founded to create public awareness of the great annual loss owing to the prevalence of tuberculosis in the city. It expanded its activities by 1911 to act as an educational vigilance organization educating the people to become aware of public health factors and in addition to support the campaign for better government.

1908   <u>Midland</u> was first published. It lasted for a few months until 1909.

June. The Fifth and Third National Banks were consolidated as the Fifth-Third National Bank.

October 25. The Mission of the Redeemer, Hyde Park, held its first services.

1909   The National Municipal League and the American Civic Association held their joint annual convention in Cincinnati.

The Visiting Nurses' Association was begun in the city.

Spring. Members of the Commerical Club, the Optimist Club, the Business Men's Club, and the Chamber of Commerce subscribed funds to establish a Bureau of Municipal Research.

May. The Western Association for the Preservation of Medical Records was established.

The Mohawk German Banking and Savings Company was organized.

June. The Commerce and Deposit Bank was organized.

July. The Evanston Bank and the Court House Savings Bank were organized.

October. The German American Commercial and Savings Bank was established.

October 8. The Episcopal clergy and laymen of the Cincinnati Convocation organized the City Mission Society.

November. Louis Schwab was elected mayor.

December. The First National and Merchants' National Banks were consolidated.

1910   The biennial convention of the Women's Club was held in Cincinnati.

1911   The Central Labor Council joined twenty-seven other civic organizations to form the United Constitutional Committee of Hamilton County to gain constitutional reforms.

June. College Hill, Mount Washington, and Saylor Park were added to Cincinnati.

July. Madisonville, Mount Airy, and Carthage were annexed.

September 5. The dam at Fern Bank was completed.

September 28 - October. The Roman Catholics held a National Eucharistic Congress in Cincinnati.

November. Henry T. Hunt was elected mayor, defeating Schwab, the Republican. He campaigned on a reform program.

1912   Three school nurses began work at twenty-eight schools in the center of the city.

1913   The Metropole Hotel was opened.

The Bureau of Catholic Charities was organized.

May 9. The street railway employees went out on strike. Strike breakers were brought in on May 11. The strike was finally settled after violence had occurred on May 19.

May 21. The Council of Social Agencies was formally incorporated.

July 2. As a result of an ice strike that had broken out in May, the city government seized six plants on the advice of the board of health. The strike was finally settled on July 6.

July 16. The trial of George B. Cox for misapplication of state funds was dismissed by Judge Caldwell.

November 4. Friedrich S. Spiegel, a Republican, was elected mayor, defeating Mayor Hunt. Other Republicans were elected as well.

August 15. An announcement was made that a hospital was to be opened in connection with the city university.

December 15. The city government announced that waterwork and sewer improvements would be begun in order to give work to the idle.

1915 G. Buchta was elected mayor.

1917 The city charter was revised providing for greater home rule.

The Cincinnati Business Women's Club was organized.

March 1. The Central Trust and Safe Deposit Company changed its name to the Central Trust Company.

September 19. The German Textbook Censoring Committee eliminated from the public schools books that strengthened ties with Germany.

May 8. The Home Guards was organized as a war emergency measure.

November 6. John Calvin, a Republican, was elected mayor.

1918 May 31. The public library removed German language newspapers and the New York American as well as the Chicago Examiner, published by William R. Hearst.

September 13. The police struck for more pay, and the Home Guard had to patrol the city. The strike was ended on September 16.

1919 September 16. The Cincinnati Reds clinched the National League pennant. It was the first pennant it had won in thirty-seven years.

October 1. Robert E. Bently Post No. 50 of the American Legion was organized.

October 9. The Cincinnati Reds won the World Series.

October 12. The Classical High School was established.

November. Mayor John Calvin was reelected.

November 18. The headquarters of the Cincinnati Socialist party was raided by the members of the American Legion, who burned the party literature.

1920 January 28. Mayor Calvin inaugurated the construction of a subway.

April 19. The United States Supreme Court upheld the Kentucky Separate Coach Act as it applied to the Cincinnati Street Railways.

1921 February 24. The City Traction Company Street Railway was enjoined from raising its fare to nine cents.

May 4. Colonel Page was chosen dean of the Cincinnati University Medical School.

July 29. The Cincinnati Times Star reduced its price.

November 8. Fred Koehler was elected mayor. The city manager form of government was accepted in a referendum.

1922 February 25. The Republican members of the city council voted to reduce their own salaries in order to aid the city's financial burden.

May 20. Union workers in the sixteen factories of the Cincinnati Boot and Shoe Manufacturers Association went out on strike.

November 19. The city government announced that it would have to cut public services because of the failure of the citizenry to vote for the tax levy. This was seen as a vote of a lack of confidence in the Republican administration of Cincinnati.

1923 January 13. Dr. E.E. North discussed plans to open a psychiatric clinic that he would head.

January 24. The Anti-Gimme League was formed to stop tipping and petty grafting.

April 26. Mr. and Mrs. Charles P. Taft donated $275,000 to Cincinnati University.

May 1. The Cincinnati Golden Jubilee Music Festival was opened.

October. The Brotherhood of Railway Clerks' National Bank was established.

November 15. The Fourth National Bank, incorporated in 1863, was merged with the Central Trust Company to become the Fourth and Central Trust Company.

December 27. Cincinnati University conferred the degree of LLD on Professor J.P. McMurrich.

1924

The Bank of Commerce and Trust Company was organized.

February 21. The Cincinnati Street Railway Company announced that it would resume operation by purchase of the leasehold and other interests of the Cincinnati Traction Company.

March 7. The Federal Trade Commission issued orders against the Cincinnati Wholesale Tobacco Association, P. Lorillard Company, Inc., the Wholesale Tobacco and Cigar Dealers' Association of Philadelphia, and the American Tobacco Company, prohibiting them from combining and cooperating for the purpose of fixing prices.

March 19. The Ladies' Auxiliary, Number 17, of the Order of Sleeping Car Conductors was organized in Cincinnati.

August 9. The city announced plans to adopt the system used by Chicago in establishing an artificial and natural service based on the extraction of gas from coal. Bonds were offered for the financing of the system on August 12.

CITY MANAGER FORM OF GOVERNMENT

1925

March 19. A special grand jury returned secret indictments involving many, for graft, in violation of the narcotic and prohibition laws. Forty-eight policemen were indicted on March 20.

May 5. The Cincinnati May Music Festival was opened by the Cincinnati Symphony.

November 4. Mrs. T.B. Samuels's story of the purchase of two children started a grand jury investigation of an alleged "baby store" in Cincinnati.

December 30. The city council, which had been elected by proportional representation, elected Murray Seasongood mayor. Col. Clarence O. Sherrill was chosen as the first city manager. The new administration was expected to end gang rule, which had been in control of various aspects of the political life of the city.

1926

January 16. Plans were announced for the erection of an office building on the site of the Burnet House.

February. The Stock Yards Bank was purchased and became the Stock Yards Branch of the Fourth and Central Trust Company.

February 3. The Salvation Army obtained a temporary injunction preventing the erection of a moving picture theater adjoining the Catherine Booth Home for Girls.

May 31. Income from the rental of the Cincinnati Southern Railway to the Cincinnati, New Orleans and Texas Pacific Railway was applied to the city's interest account. The city was the owner of the railway.

June 19. An announcement was made that the police would carry cameras to aid them in detecting and preventing crime.

August 5. The city council employed J.A. Beelor to make a traffic survey.

November 1. Arthur Nash hired detectives to guard against election frauds. Members of the Amalgamated Clothing Workers of America announced their plans to aid as well.

December 16. Plans were announced for a "Hill of Remembrance" as a war memorial.

December 24. Directors of the Fifth-Third National Bank and the Union Trust Company voted to consolidate the two banks.

1927

January 24. The Board of Education struck Woodrow Wilson's name from the list of "immortals" for the new school building after the students had voted to include it.

January 25. The Cincinnati rail depot was innundated by rising flood waters.

June 1. Mr. and Mrs. Charles P. Taft donated their home, art collection, and $1,000,000 to the Cincinnati Institute of Fine Arts.

November 8. The voters decided to extend the lease of the Cincinnati Southern Railroad for an additional sixty years to the Cincinnati, New Orleans and Texas Pacific Railway.

A nonpartisan city administration was elected, ending the rule of Fred Schneller's group.

November 22. An announcement was made of a gift of J. N. Gamble to found a Medical Institute.

December 9. Jacob G. Schmidlapp left a trust fund to establish a chair of aviation at the University of Cincinnati.

1928

The General Electric Company announced plans for construction of the largest automatic power supply system in the world in order to help supply the street railways of Cincinnati.

April 10. The formation of the Cincinnati Gas and Electric Company by the merger of the Cincinnati Gas and Electric Company with the Columbia Power Company was approved.

May 9. The purchase of the Union Gas and Electric Company by the Cincinnati Gas and Electric Company was approved.

November 14. Funds were raised to endow the Cincinnati Institute of Fine Arts.

November 24. The city was enjoined from proceeding with its street widening program.

1929

January 19. The city government announced plans for a radio net to aid the police in the capture of criminals.

1930

March 10. The Taft Memorial Beacon Tower was proposed for Alms Park.

May 1. Ulysses S. Grant, III refused the offer to become the city manager.

May 7. Mrs. Charles P. Taft gave a gift of $2,000,000 to aid the study of humanities as a memorial to her husband at the University of Cincinnati.

July. Col. Clarence O. Sherril was succeeded as city manager by Clarence A. Dykstra of Los Angeles.

July 14. Miss B. Bauer donated money to establish the Cincinnati Conservatory of Music as part of the Cincinnati Institute of Fine Arts.

December 4. The <u>Cincinnati Enquirer</u> bought the <u>Cincinnati Commercial Tribune</u> and then suspended its operations. The former was the only morning paper in the city.

December 14. The city announced plans to establish a worker-manager council as part of the city government.

1932

January 2. A compulsory pension system for city employees went into effect.

March 28. The bonds of the Cincinnati Union Terminal Company were admitted to the New York Stock Exchange list.

September 17. The occupational tax was abolished.

1933

March 20. The city code was reenacted.

May 20. Students of the University of Cincinnati organized a protest against the suppression of free speech and academic freedom and discrimination against the Jews by the National Socialist government in German colleges and universities.

September 5. Receivers of the Cincinnati and Lake Erie Railroad Company were allowed to cut fares on the Cincinnati-Dayton division in half.

November 7. The Charter ticket won elections, although the results took several days to be verified.

December 16. The Cincinnati Symphony Orchestra announced plans to give the world premiere of E. Whithorne's First Symphony.

1934	January. Russell Willson was elected mayor.

November 5. The Supreme Court upheld Cincinnati's right to a five cent fare on the Newport and Covington Railway.

December 12. The city announced plans to offer a bond issue. |
| 1935 | March 11. Cincinnati bought the Georgetown and Portsmouth Railroad.

October 30. J.K. Lilly presented his Stephen C. Foster memorabilia to the University of Cincinnati.

November 12. The Cincinnati bond issue was awarded. |
| 1936 | January 8. Mayor Russell Willson was reelected mayor after the council had been deadlocked.

May 12. Proportional representation was retained by the voters in a referendum.

May 14. The Interstate Commerce Commission authorized a bond issue for the Cincinnati Union Terminal Company.

May 30. The Cincinnati Art Museum celebrated the fiftieth anniversary of its dedication.

June 17. The school district bonds were awarded.

July 1. The Federal Power Commission approved the merger of the Cincinnati Gas and Electric Company as the Union Gas and Electric Company.

December 9. The New York Stock Exchange approved the listing of bonds of the Cincinnati Gas and Electric Company. |
1937	June 15. Col. Clarence O. Sherrill accepted reappointment as city manager.
1938	January 1. James Garfield Stewart, Republican, was elected mayor by the city council.
1939	September 28. The Cincinnati Reds clinched the National League pennant.

CHRONOLOGY

October 8. The New York Yankees defeated the Cincinnati Reds 4-0 to win the World Series.

November 8. Mayor James Stewart was reelected by the city council.

1940   September 18. The Cincinnati Reds clinched the National League pennant.

October 8. Cincinnati won the World Series, defeating Detroit in the seventh game.

October 21. Stockholders of the Cincinnati Street Railway Company voted to accept a city franchise.

1941   June 7. The _Cincinnati Enquirer_ marked its one hundredth anniversary with a special centenary edition.

1942   January 17. Students of the University of Cincinnati started a paper saving campaign.

September 11. The Cincinnati Planer Company received permission of the OPA (Office of Price Administration) to charge higher prices for boring mills and parts.

1943   March 5. The Cincinnati _Times-Star_ began its V-Mail edition.

November 5. The Cincinnati Observatory celebrated its centennial.

1944   March 11. The University of Cincinnati announced plans for lectures on postwar city planning problems.

September 19. The city government announced plans to purchase the Cincinnati Gas and Electric Company from the parent Columbia Gas and Electric Corporation.

1945   James G. Stewart was elected mayor.

March 12. The University of Cincinnati formed a veterans guidance office to aid the soldiers returning after the war.

1946   September 21. The Evening College of the University of Cincinnati expanded to meet the adult education needs of the city.

November 16. The Cincinnati *Times Star* raised its prices.

November 18. The Cincinnati *Enquirer* raised its prices.

1947

March 6. Carl W. Rich was named mayor, succeeding James G. Stewart who resigned to become a Justice of the Ohio Supreme Court.

March 12. The Columbia Gas and Electric Company sold its interest in the Cincinnati Gas and Electric Company to the city.

June 7. The Evening College of the University of Cincinnati offered a Bachelor of Industrial Management degree program.

August 2. The International Astronomical Union designated the University of Cincinnati Observatory as a world clearinghouse for information on asteroids.

August 3. The Industrial Health Institute announced that it would offer the first two-year postgraduate course for the Doctor of Industrial Medicine degree.

November 2. In the city election the primary system was retained.

1948

January 1. Democrat Albert D. Cash was elected mayor because Councilman Taft refused to back the Republican nominee. He was the first Democratic mayor since 1913.

January 12. The United Corporation announced that it would buy the stock of the Cincinnati Gas and Electric Company with an SEC permit.

1950

The population of Cincinnati was 503,998.

January 2. Mayor Cash was reelected by the city council.

February 16. The Giddings and Lewis Machine Tool Company absorbed the Cincinnati Planer Company.

February 23. The Ohio Supreme Court ruled that the Cincinnati Gas and Electric Company's 6 percent return on its operation was reasonable and denied the city of Cincinnati's motion for lower rates.

CHRONOLOGY

1951   June 20. The Ohio Supreme Court upheld the primary system for electing councilmen in Cincinnati.

August 1. The Cincinnati health service announced development of a filter to speed germ content analysis. It helped to cut water-borne disease in rural areas.

August 2. The city council opened a probe into alleged kickbacks to the police by tow car operators, professional bondsmen, and bookmakers.

August 8. As a result of the suspension of forty-five policemen for graft, the police department was put on a forty-eight-hour week.

September 22. The Evening College of the University of Cincinnati offered a graduate engineering program for the first time.

October 18. H.A. Garcia was the first black student admitted to the Cincinnati Conservatory of Music.

November 13. The Cincinnati *Record* ceased publication.

December 1. Carl W. Rich was elected mayor.

1952   June 6. After much wrangling in which the Taft family, owners of the *Times-Star,* tried to purchase the Cincinnati *Enquirer*, the United States District Court approved sale of the paper to the Portsmouth Steel Corporation, which had a collateral agreement to sell the *Enquirer* to the employees of the paper.

September 30. The employees of the *Enquirer* completed their arrangements for purchase of the paper from the Portsmouth Steel Company. Funds were to be obtained by a bond issue.

October 17. The Atomic Energy Commission reported that eleven companies, including the Cincinnati Gas and Electric Company, would associate with Dow Chemical and Detroit Edison project to develop a power reactor for the Ohio Valley area.

1953   Mayor Waldvogel was elected.

July 17. President Eisenhower signed a bill authorizing the Atomic Energy Commission to negotiate a twenty-five-year electrical contract with the Ohio Valley Electric Corporation with a cancellation clause. The Cincinnati Gas and Electric Company was one of the participating utility companies.

October 5. Planning Commission Director Williams resigned at the request of the city because he had attended a Marxist study group in 1946.

October 26. The Cincinnati Enquirer declared the first dividend under employee ownership.

November 25. City Manager Kellogg resigned.

1954

February 10. The city council approved a payroll tax to meet a $7 million deficit.

March 10. Charles Adair Harrell was appointed city manager.

May 7. Mayor Waldvogel died. Vice Mayor Dolby became acting mayor.

November 3. A city referendum was held that repealed the primary system and approved a new system by which a voter had six votes for the nine-member city council. A recount was called for.

November 10. Carl W. Rich was elected mayor.

November 19. A recount of the primary indicated a reversal of the votes by 790 votes. Therefore the primary system for selecting councilmen was retained.

1955

February 12. The Cincinnati Transit Company reported its first guaranteed seat-express ride service for suburban commuters was successful and would be extended.

July 27. Mrs. Cash was elected Charter Committee president.

August 28. The Cincinnati Milling Machine Company was bought by the Heald Machine Company.

November 24. The Cincinnati Rubber Manufacturing Company was sold to the Thor Power Tool Company.

December 14. Charles Phelps Taft was named mayor and Theodore M. Berry, vice mayor.

1956 March 7. The city council rejected a petition for a referendum on the ending of the primary system of electing the members of the council. It charged fraudulent signatures on the petition.

1957 April 20. The Cincinnati Enquirer raised its price from five cents to seven cents. The Cincinnati Post and Times-Star did the same.

September 30. The Republicans were successful in the special election to end the primary system of electing the city council members.

November 6. Mayor Taft won reelection to the city council, but Vice Mayor Berry was defeated.

December 1. The Republican-dominated city council elected Donald D. Clancy mayor and William C. Kelly, vice mayor.

1958 April 23. The Cincinnati Reds signed a five-year pact to stay in the city. The city agreed to increase additional off-street parking.

September 6. City Manager Harrell described plans to keep the downtown property values high by improving the area and cutting traffic congestion.

September 18. The city public library banned Vladimir Nabokov's Lolita.

1959 January 10. The thirty-four-year old Democratic-Independent-Republican Coalition, which worked through the City Charter Commission, ended, as the Democrats planned their own slate for the November election.

1960 The population of Cincinnati was 502,550.

1961 January 5. The city council elected Vice Mayor Walton H. Bachrach mayor.

March 11. A redevelopment project for light industry was planned near the Ohio River.

April 7. The late Mrs. Semple left a $3 million trust fund to develop a classics department at the University of Cincinnati. It was the largest gift in the university's history.

August 2. The Cincinnati College Conservatory of Music announced plans to merge with the University of Cincinnati in 1962.

September 26. The Cincinnati Reds won the National League pennant.

October 9. The Cincinnati Reds were defeated in the World Series by the New York Yankees, 4-1.

December 2. Walton H. Bachrach was reelected mayor.

1962

June 23. The University of Cincinnati offered a new doctoral program stressing the philosophical and moral implications of psychiatry.

August 8. The Cincinnati Gas and Electric Company bought a jet engine to power a generator unit.

September 22. The city council voted approval of the downtown renewal plan, awarding the contract to the Emery Knutson Development Company.

September 29. The Cincinnati *Enquirer* announced a rise in its price from seven cents to ten cents.

1963

September 3. Blacks and whites, in separate demonstrations, picketed the Cincinnati public school system in a dispute over transfer of blacks to an all-white grade school.

November 1. The downtown redevelopment project that threatened legitimate theater spurred a campaign of business and civic leaders, which revitalized the theater and increased downtown business.

November 6. The Republicans retained control of the city council.

December 24. A code of ethics for civil employees was adopted.

CHRONOLOGY 63

1964   January 4. Civil rights groups sued the Cincinnati Board of Education over de facto segregation and requested a federal court to bar the building of a new public school because it would further segregation.

May 9. The Cincinnati CORE chapter proposed the creation of five to six "education centers" in the city to help solve the desegregation controversy.

May 27. The Justice Department sued to make the Scripps-Howard chain divest itself of the Cincinnati <u>Enquirer</u>, charging that the 1956 acquisition by Scripps, which also owned the Cincinnati <u>Post</u> and <u>Times-Star</u>, violated the antitrust laws by depriving readers and advertisers of free competition. This suit was the first in the newspaper field.

1965   December 9. The Cincinnati Gas and Electric, Columbus and Southern Ohio and Dayton Power and Light companies announced plans for building on the Ohio River, fifty miles east of Cincinnati, what would become one of the world's largest steam-generating plants.

1966   October 24. The Cincinnati Center Renewal Project received a $20 million mortgage loan.

December 5. The Cincinnati Reds were sold to a local investors group called 617 Inc. for a reported $7 million. The Cincinnati <u>Enquirer</u> was among the group, with its publisher, Francis K. Dale, to be temporary president. The deal was to be completed in January, 1967, when the name of the new corporation would be changed to the Cincinnati Reds, Inc.

December 6. The United States Appeal Court ruled that the Cincinnati school board did not have to bus pupils to prevent segregation. A motion was filed by a local black group backed by the NAACP, which led to remanding the case to a federal court for further ruling on other disputed issues.

1967   March 1. M. Johnson bequeathed his $2 million modern art collection to the Cincinnati Art Museum.

June 12. Rioting broke out in the black Avondale section. Governor Rhodes sent in 800 National Guardsmen at the request of Mayor Bachrach. The National Guard troops remained in the area for a few days to maintain order and finally withdrew on June 18.

July 3. New disturbances occurred in the Avondale section. At one point firemen were attacked. The area was finally calmed on July 6.

October 31. The Amalgamated Transit bus drivers struck the Cincinnati Transit Company in the first transit strike in the city's history. The strike ended on December 7 when the drivers accepted a three-year contract providing a fifty-cent per hour wage rise.

November 11. A multimillion-dollar building development program was planned in Avondale to offer employment and training for the disadvantaged. It was to include housing and a shopping center, as well as community, educational, and recreational facilities. This was done as a result of the summer disturbances.

December 1. Vice Mayor Eugene P. Ruehlmann was elected mayor by the city council.

1968

February 13. City Manager William C. Wichman resigned amid rumors that the city council Republicans were planning to remove him.

April 3. William McClain was named acting city manager. This was the highest executive post ever held by a black in the city's history.

April 8. National Guardsmen quelled disorders in the black section of Avondale that followed a false rumor that police had killed a black woman. The woman was killed as a result of a gun battle between rioters and a private store guard. Disorders occurred following a memorial service for the late Rev. Dr. Martin Luther King, Jr. The city imposed a curfew, which was lifted on April 10.

April 17. The city council passed an antiriot law giving the mayor and city manager the power to declare a state of emergency, and take certain emergency actions.

August 16. Racial violence broke out in the black Avondale section. A youth was shot by policemen after throwing bottles at officers, and a black woman was killed after being shot from a passing car. Several men were held in the shooting and were charged with murder on August 17.

1969

January 15. City employees demanding more pay in state, county, and municipal offices, struck in defiance of a court injunction.

December 1. Republican Mayor Eugene P. Ruehlmann was reelected.

December 20. Calvin H. Canliffe was appointed to head the board of education. He was the first black to hold the position.

1970

The population of Cincinnati was 452,524.

January 5. Twelve hundred nonuniformed employees struck over wage demands. The city agreed to a pact, which ended the strike on February 5 with a 7 percent average wage increase granted.

DOCUMENTS

The documents in this section have been carefully selected to illustrate the social, political, commercial, and cultural life of Cincinnati from the late eighteenth century through the 1960s. The most pertinent items from the ordinances, charters and reports of the various agencies of the city were chosen in order to indicate the major changes that have occurred in the governance of Cincinnati. Especially important in this area is the experiment in the city-manager form of government, which has continued to this day. In addition, documents pertaining to the reform of municipal politics have been included. The importance of city planning, which was recognized in Cincinnati as early as the second decade of the twentieth century, is indicated by various proposals on roads, urban renewal, housing, recreational facilities, and downtown redevelopment. The complete documents may be studied in the sources mentioned at the end of the introduction to each of them. Obviously much more could have been included, but the most important documents were selected due to the limited space.

INAUGURATION OF RIVER TRAFFIC BETWEEN
CINCINNATI AND PITTSBURGH, 1794

Cincinnati had been determined to utilize the river as a valuable contribution to its commercial growth. Therefore the citizens received the news of the beginning of packet service on the river between Cincinnati and Pittsburgh with great interest and excitement. This advertisement reproduced by Charles Goss from the Centinel of the Northwest Territory on January 11, 1974 indicates the type of service and the regulations involved.

Source: Charles Frederic Goss. Cincinnati, The Queen City, 1788-1912. Cincinnati, 1912. vol. II, pp. 93-94.

The Centinel of the Northwest Territory, January 11, 1794 carried the first advertisement in regard to river traffic between Cincinnati and Pittsburgh.

"OHIO PACKET BOATS.

"Two boats, for the present, will start from Cincinnati to Pittsburgh, and return to Concinnati, in the following manner, viz.:

"First boat will leave Cincinnati this morning at eight o'clock, and return to Cincinnati, so as to be ready to sail again in four weeks from this date.

"Second boat will leave Cincinnati on Saturday, the 30th instant, and return to Cincinnati as above.

"And so, regularly, each boat performing the voyage to and from Cincinnati and Pittsburgh, once in every four weeks.

"Two boats, in addition to the above, will shortly be completed in such a manner that one boat of the line will set out weekly from Cincinnati to Pittsburgh, and return to Cincinnati in like manner.

"The proprietors of these boats having maturely considered the many inconveniences and dangers incident to the common method hitherto adopted of navigating the Ohio, and being influenced by a love of philanthrophy and a desire of being serviceable to the public, has taken great pains to render the accommodations on board the boats as agreeable and convenient as they could possibly be made.

"No danger need be apprehended from the enemy, as every person on board will be under cover, made proof to rifle or musket balls, and convenient port holes for firing out. Each of the boats is armed with six pieces, carrying a pound ball; also a good number of muskets and amply supplied with plenty of ammunition, strongly manned with choice hands, and the master of approved knowledge.

"A separate cabin from that designed for the men is partitioned off in each boat for accommodating ladies on their passage. Conveniences are constructed on board each boat so as to render landing unneccessary, as it might, at times, be attended with danger.

"Rules and regulations for maintaining order on board, and for the good management of the boats, and tables accurately calculated for the rates of freightage for passengers and carriage of letters to and from Cincinnati to Pittsburgh; also a table of the arrival and departure to and from the different places on the Ohio, between Cincinnati and Pittsburgh, may be seen on board each boat, and at the printing office in Cincinnati.

"Passengers will be supplied with provisions and liquors of all kinds, of the first quality, as the most reasonable rates possible. Persons desirous of working their passage will be admitted, on finding themselves subject, however, to the same order and direction, from the master of the boats, as the rest of the working hands of the boat's crew.

"An office of insurance will be kept at Cincinnati, Limestone, and Pittsburgh, where persons desirous of having their property insured may apply. The rates of insurance will be moderate."

FIRE DEPARTMENT REGULATIONS, EARLY NINETEENTH CENTURY

Cincinnati enacted its first legislation in regard to firefighting in 1802. C.F. Goss cited the following regulations: "Every freeholder and every person being a householder and paying an annual rent as high as thirty-six dollars must be provided with a blackjack and leather bucket of a capacity of two and one-half gallons and contribute the use of it and his own physical exertions whenever he should hear a cry of fire. Every male between sixteen and fifty years of age had to serve. Such was the first step for fire protection in Cincinnati that was to produce the first fire engine to be operated by steam -- a blessing that the entire world now appreciates."

The revised ordinance printed below indicates the problems faced by burgeoning cities such as Cincinnati in regard to fires and the careful attention to detail paid by the city government. The fire companies to be registered within the Department were to be permitted to develop their own governmental structure.

Sources: Charles Frederic Goss. Cincinnati, The Queen City, 1788-1912. Cincinnati, 1912. vol. II, p. 59. Digest of the Laws and Ordinances of Cincinnati, of a General Nature, Now in Force. Cincinnati, 1842, pp. 69-72.

FIRE DEPARTMENT

An ordinance for preventing and extinguishing Fires, and to regulate the keeping of Gun Powder; also, to prevent the erection of Wooden Buildings within certain limits.

1. Sec. I. Be it ordained by the city council of the city of Cincinnati, That the fire warden company, No. 1, and the several fire engine companies, to wit: No. 1, No. 2, No. 3, and No. 4, and the hook and ladder company, No. 1, and the hose company No. 1, and all other engine companies that may be hereafter formed, and accepted by the city council, shall be entitled to receive a certificate of membership, individually, from the clerk of the city council, which certificate may be properly adduced as evidence of their right to the privilege of the 9th section of the city charter, exempting firemen from military duty. And each of the above named companies, and such other companies as may be hereafter accepted by the city council, may form a constitution, and enact such by-laws, to be enforced under such penalties for the regulation and prompt attendance of their own company as a majority of said company think proper; (provided such by-laws are not repugnant to the laws of this city, this state, or the United States,) and all fines and penalties incurred by any fireman, for the violation of any of the by-laws thus

made, may be recovered by prosecution before the mayor, and all fines or forfeitures, so collected, shall be paid to the foreman of the company in which the forfeit was made, for the benefit of the said company.

2. Sec. II. That when any of the aforesaid companies shall be disbanded, or when new companies shall become necessary, volunteers may offer, by enrolling themselves into a company, choosing a foreman and secretary, and reporting their names to the city council for acceptance, their number being limited by the city council: But from the consideration that practice and long experience approach towards perfection, it is considered inexpedient to make annual or frequent changes in the members of the fire department, but that they should hold their appointments during the pleasure of the city council: Provided, however, that all companies belonging to the fire department, and each individual composing those companies, shall be subject to the control of the city council, and whole companies or individuals shall be liable to be displaced for any improper conduct, or when the public interest may require a change, and successors appointed.

3. Sec. III. Repealed.

4. Sec. IV. That the fire wardens are hereby authorized to enter any house or building, lot, yard, or premises, in this city, between sun rising and setting, on any week day, for the purpose of examining any fire-places, hearths, chimneys, stoves, or stove pipes, ovens, boilers, kettles, or other apparatus or fixtures, which may be dangerous in causing or promoting fires; and when any danger shall appear from any apparatus as aforesaid, of fires taking place, they shall, or any of them may direct, in writing, the owner, agent, or occupant of any premises containing any of the dangers aforesaid, to remove, alter, or amend the same, in such manner and within such time, as they or either of them may deem reasonable and just; and any person or persons who shall resist the entrance of the fire wardens as aforesaid, into any premises as aforesaid, or shall neglect or refuse to attend to the directions given for altering, amending, or removing any of the dangers aforesaid, shall forfeit and pay for every such offence, any sum not exceeding fifty dollars to be recovered before the mayor, with costs of suit, and the further sum of five dollars, to be recovered before the mayor with costs of suit, for every day they shall suffer the same to remain, after reasonable time given as aforesaid.

5. Sec. V. That it shall be the duty of all persons hereafter building any hearth, or hearths, within the boundaries of the corporation, to construct the same on a stone or brick arch, and in all cases where the back of the fire place shall be three feet or more wide, the hearth shall extend at least twenty-four inches in front beyond the jambs; and where the back of the fire-place shall be less than three feet wide, the hearth shall extend not less than twenty-two inches in front beyond the jambs.

6. Sec. VI. That it shall be the duty of all persons using a tight stove, or stoves, in any house, store, shop, or building, within the corporation, to have a platform of stone, brick, sheet iron, or earth, under the said stove or stoves, extending at least six inches in every direction

beyond that part of the lower plate that fronts the door of said stove or stoves; and that all stove pipes, at their intersection with any floor, partition, roof, or side of a house through which they pass, shall be made to pass through a crock, or if through a window it shall be enclosed with tin; and all chimneys shall in all cases extend at least two feet and a half beyond the roof or side of a house through which it passes, and if through the side of a house, it shall be capped with a cross pipe not less than eighteen inches in length, and no person shall be permitted to place a stove pipe through any building so as to project into the street: Provided, nevertheless, that if, from any peculiar circumstances, it should be the opinion of any three of the fire wardens as aforesaid, that further precautions are necessary beyond what are defined in the fifth and sixth sections of this ordinance, they may give such further directions as to them the circumstances of the case may seem to require, and their directions shall be considered lawful; and any person or persons offending against any of the provisions of this or the preceding section, shall be fined in any sum not exceeding twenty dollars, and not less than five dollars, with costs of suit, on conviction thereof before the mayor.

DESCRIPTION OF CINCINNATI, EARLY NINETEENTH CENTURY

Dr. Daniel Drake, who was to be a major contributor, albeit controversial figure, in the development of the field of medical education, had arrived in Cincinnati in 1800. His description of the city at that time, as expressed in a speech in 1852, presents a picture of the town with its residences, business, and other institutions.

Source: Charles Frederic Goss. <u>Cincinnati, The Queen City, 1788-1912</u>. Cincinnati, 1912, vol. I, pp. 86-89.

In the first year of this century, the cleared lands at this place (Cincinnati) did not equal the surface which is now completely built over. North of the Canal and west of the Western Row there was forest, with here and there a cabin and small clearing, connected with the village by a narrow, winding road. Curved lines, you know, symbolize the country, straight lines, the city. South of where the Commercial Hospital now administers relief annually to three times as many people as then composed the population of the town, there were half cleared fields, with broad margins of blackberry vines; and I, with other young persons, frequently gathered that delicious fruit at the risk of being snake bitten where the Roman Catholic Cathedral now sends its spire into the lower clouds. Further south, the ancient mound near Fifth Street on which General Wayne planted his sentinels seven years before, was overshadowed with trees which, together with itself, should have been preserved; but its dust, like that of those who there delighted to play upon its slopes, has mingled with the remains of the unknown race by whom it was erected. The very spot on which we are now assembled (6th and Vine) but a few years before the time of which I speak, was part of a wheat field of sixteen acres owned by Mr. James Ferguson and fenced in without reference to the paved streets which now cut through it.

The stubble of that field is still decaying in the soil around the foundations of the noble edifice in which we are now assembled. Seventh Street, then called Northern Row, was almost the northern limit of population. Sixth Street had a few scattering houses; Fifth, not many more. Between that and Fourth there was a public square, now built over. In one corner, the northeast, stood the Court House, with a small market place in front, which nobody attended. In the northwest corner was the jail, in the southwest, the village schoolhouse; in the southeast, where a glittering spire tells the stranger that he is approaching our city, stood the humble church of the pioneers, whose bones lie mouldering in the center of the Square, then the village cemetery. Walnut, called Cider Street, which bounds that Square on the west, presented a few cabins or small frames; but Vine street was not yet opened to the river. Fourth Street, after passing Vine, branched into roads and paths. Third

Street, running near the brow of the upper plain, was on as high a level as Fifth Street is now. The gravelly slope of that plain stretched from east to west almost to Pearl Street. On this slope, between Main and Walnut, a French political exile whom I shall name hereafter planted, in the latter part of the last century, a small vineyard. This was the beginning of that cultivation for which the environs of our city have at last become distinguished. I suppose this was the first cultivation of the foreign grape in the Valley of the Ohio. Where Congress, Market and Pear Streets since opened, send up the smoke of their great iron foundries, or display in magnificient warehouses the products of different and distant lands, there was a belt of low, wet ground which, up to the settlement of the town twelve years before, has been a series of beaver ponds, filled by the annual overflow of the river and the rains from the upper plains. Second, then known as Columbia Street, presented some scattered cabins, dirty within and rude without; but Front Street presented an aspect of considerable pretension. It was nearly built with log and frame houses, from Walnut Street to Eastern Row now called Broadway. The people of wealth and the men of business, with the Hotel de Ville, kept by Griffin Yeatman, were chiefly on this street, which even had a few patches of sidewalk pavement. In front of the mouth of Sycamore Street, near the hotel, there was a small market house built over a cove into which piroques and other craft, when the river was high, were poled or paddled to be tied to the rude columns.

The Commons then stretched out to where the land and water now meet, when the river is at its mean height. It terminated in a high, steep, crumbling bank beneath which lay the flat boats of the immigrants or traders in flour, whiskey and apples from Wheeling, Fort Pitt, or Red Stone Old Fort. Their winter fires burning in iron kettles, sent up lazy columns of smoke, where steamers now darken the air with hurried clouds of steam and soot. One of these vessels has cost more than the village would have then brought at auction! From this Common the future Covington in Kentucky appeared as a corn field, cultivated by the Kennedy family, which also kept the ferry. Newport, chiefly owned by two Virginia gentlemen, James Taylor and Richard Southgate, but embracing the Majors, Fowlers, Berrys, Stubbs and several other respectable families, was a drowsy village set in the side of a deep wood, and the mouth of the Licking River was over-arched with trees, giving it the appearance of a great tunnel.

After Front Street, Sycamore and Main were the most important streets of the town. A number of homes were built upon the former up to Fourth, beyond which it was opened three of four squares. The buildings and business of Main Street were on the northwest corner where there was a brick house owned by Elmore Williams, the only one in town. Beyond Seventh, Main Street was a mere road, nearly impassable in muddy weather, which at the foot of the hills divided into two, called the Hamilton Road and the Mad River Road. The former, now a crooked and closely built street, took the course of the Brighton House; the latter made a steep ascent over Mount Auburn, where there was not a single habitation. Broadway, or Eastern Row, was but thirty-three feet wide. The few buildings which it had were on the west side where it joins Front street; on the site of the Cincinnati Hotel there was a low frame house with whiskey and a billard table. It was said that the owner paid $700.00 for the house and lot in "nine pences;" that is, small pieces of "cut money" received from Indians. North of this, toward Second Street, there was several small houses inhabited by disorderly persons who had been in the army. The Sidewalk in front was called Battle Row. Between Second and Third Streets near where we now have the eastern end of the market place, there was a single frame tenement in which I lived with my preceptor, Dr. Epworth, in 1805. In a pond directly in front, the frogs gave us regular serenades. Much of the square to which this house belonged was fenced in and served as a pasture ground for a pony which I kept for country practice.

Between Third and Fourth Streets, on the west side of Broadway, there was in 1800 a cornfield, with a rude cornfield fence, since replaced by mansions of such magnificence that a Russian traveler, several years ago, took away drawings of one as a model for the people of St. Petersburg. Above Fourth Street, Broadway had but two or three houses and terminated at the edge of a thick wood before reaching the foot of Mount Auburn.

East of Broadway and north of Fourth Street, the entire square had been enclosed, and a respectable frame house erected by the Hon. Winthrop Sargent, Secretary of the Northwest. He had removed to Mississippi territory, of which he was afterwards Governor; and his house and grounds the best improved in the village, were occupied by Charles Williams Bird, his successor in office. Governor Sargent merits a notice among the physicians of the town as he was the first who made scientific observations on our climate.

Immediately south of his residence from Fourth Street to the river east of Broadway, there was a military reserve. That portion of it which laid on the upper plain was covered by Fort Washington with its bastions, port holes, stockades, tall flag staff, evening tattoo and morning reveille. Here were the quarters of the military members of our profession and for a time, one of its civil members also, for after its evacuation in 1803 my preceptor moved into the rooms which had been occupied by the commander of the post. . . .

POSTAL SYSTEM, EARLY NINETEENTH CENTURY

A post office was first established at nearby Chillicothe in 1799 and soon was extended to serve Cincinnati as well. Charles Goss presents a description of the growing postal service in Cincinnati, utilizing various newspaper accounts. This indicates something of the growth of Cincinnati as well as its contacts with distant parts of the country.

Source: Charles Frederic Goss. Cincinnati, The Queen City, 1788-1912. Cincinnati, 1912, vol II, pp. 120-122.

On May 17, 1799, the Western Spy and Hamilton Gazette announced: "Post-office. -- Notice is hereby given that a post office is established at Chillicothe. The persons, therefore having business in that part of the country may have speedy and safe conveyance by post for letters, packets, &c." That mail was then taken on horseback, following an Indian trail.

The same paper stated March 12, 1800, that a post route had been opened between Louisville and Kaskaskia, also one between Nashville and Natchez. "This will open an easy channel of communication with those remote places, which has heretofore been extremely difficult, particularly from the Atlantic States."

The mail carrier from Louisville was compelled to carry food for himself and horse from Louisville to Cincinnati. His path lay all the way through woods, where he was exposed to perils from animals and Indians as well as to hunger.

The Daily Commercial, Cincinnati, December, 1874, gave some reminiscences of this period in an interview: "In 1808-09 Peter Williams had contracts for carrying the mails between Louisville and Cincinnati, Cincinnati and Lexington, Cincinnati and Chillicothe, and Cincinnati and Greenville in Drake county. All these contracts were performed with pack horses through the dense forests and along the 'blazed' tracks or paths which, in those days, were called roads. The trip from Cincinnati to Louisville was generally performed in about two weeks' time. The provender for the horses had frequently to be carried along, it being impossible to procure any on the way. So of the other routes to the different places named, -- everywhere through the grand dense forests, filled with wild game of all kinds. Our informant recollects many rude incidents which occurred on many trips he, as a boy, made with his father, and afterwards by himself, as he became older, to Chillicothe, Greenville, Louisville, &c. Mr. Williams retained these mail contracts up to 1821, using pack horses during the whole time, and only releasing them on the advent of the stage coaches, owners of which could afford to carry the mails at about one half the price he was getting. In those early days the pack horse was the only way in which supplies of every kind could be transported any distance; and Mr. Williams distinctly remembers that his father possessed the only wagon in the country around Cincinnati, and that, being of no use, was suffered to rot down in the barn."

Samuel Lewis was one of the youthful carriers of mail employed by Mr. Williams. His son said in an account of his life: "After working a short time upon the farm, he was employed in carrying the United States mail, for which Mr. Williams had a contract at that time. His route was at first from Cincinnati to Williamsburg, and afterward from the latter point to Chillicothe. This work often required seven days and two nights in the week, making the labor very severe. In addition to this, the creeks and small rivers along the route were to be forded, bridges at that period being out of the question. This was all done on horseback. The routes covered most of the country east of Cincinnati to the Scioto river at Chillicothe, and southward of this to the Ohio river, including Maysville, Kentucky.

"Over some of these streams, during high water, it was necessary to swim the horse; while often the attempt was accompanied with much danger. At one time, being compelled to swim his horse, he had secured the mail bag, as he supposed, and commenced crossing the stream, swimming himself and leading the horse. When nearly over, the mail bag from some cause became unloosed and floated off. His horse was first to be secured, and then the mail. Its recovery and the renewal of his journey would have been speedy, but he was struck by a floating log and severely injured. Making his way with extreme difficulty to the shore, he succeeded in mounting his horse and continuing his journey to the next town, which he reached completely drenched and exhausted, and where he remained for some days before he was able to renew his round. The accident unfitted him for his employment for the time, and when he returned to Cincinnati he was occupied with other labor."

Mr. Lewis afterward became a distinguished man, was largely influential in the founding of the two greatest high schools of the city, and was the first superintendent of public schools in this state.

January 1st, 1815, William Burke became postmaster. He was commonly called "Father Burke," was a Methodist itinerent preacher and had been presiding elder. Mr. Mansfield states that Burke was a southerner: "He seemed to have lost his voice and always spoke low and in guttural tones. He was always chewing tobacco and, being a postmaster, was always a democrat. He was a strong Methodist and seemed an amiable man." Burke separated himself from his denomination, procured a place of worship for his followers, and often preached there. He was inclined to politics, was at first a Jeffersonian and then a Jackson democrat. He held office until the whigs came into power. Burke had as his assistant for a long time Elam P. Langdon, who also maintained the Cincinnati Reading Room, where many newspapers and journals, American and foreign, could be consulted. The postoffice in 1819 was at 157 Main street.

April 13th, 1841, President Tyler appointed as postmaster W.H.H. Taylor, who removed the office to Main street above Columbia or Second street; subsequently he chose a site on Main street near Fourth.

The number of mails to and from Cincinnati in 1826 was twenty each week. A portion of these was carried on ten stage coaches, three on the Chillicothe route, three on the Lebanon, three on the Dayton and Columbus route, and one on that to Georgetown, Kentucky. Ten mails were conveyed by postriders.

In 1826 the income of the Cincinnati postoffice from postage was eight thousand, one hundred and odd dollars. There were delivered in that year three thousand, seven hundred and fifty free letters.

Early in 1827 another line of stage coaches was started by way of Xenia, Urbana, Maysville, and Bucyrus to Lower Sandusky. At Sandusky the mail was put on a boat, and by this change letters reached New York in ten days. A daily line was also run to Wheeling, reaching Baltimore in eight or nine days; this route was almost the same as that taken later by the National pike. Stages at this time also were run from Cincinnati to Lexington, eighty miles.

In 1828-29 the income of the Cincinnati postoffice was twelve thousand, one hundred and fifty dollars, an increase of fifty per cent in three years. Twenty-three mails came and went each week, eighteen by stages and five by horseback.

In 1829-30 the income was sixteen thousand, two hundred and fifty odd dollars. In this latter year, sixty-four mails came and went each week. Of these, thirty-six were by stages, eleven on horseback, ten on steamboats, and seven part way by steamboat and partly by land. . . .

ESTABLISHMENT OF CINCINNATI WATER SUPPLY
March 31, 1817

As Cincinnati began to grow, the use of wells for a water supply was no longer sufficient. Therefore the city government passed an ordinance giving the exclusive privilege of supplying water to the city to the Cincinnati Manufacturing Company for ninety-nine years. This was the beginning of the important water supply system.

Source: <u>An Act Incorporating the City of Cincinnati and the Ordinance of Said City Now in Force</u>. Cincinnati, January, 1928.

AN ORDINANCE
FOR SUPPLYING THE TOWN OF CINCINNATI WITH WATER.

Sec. 1. <u>Be it ordained by the Town Council of the Town of Cincinnati</u>, That the Cincinnati Manufacturing Company, their heirs, successors and assigns, shall be, and they are hereby vested with the exclusive privilege of conveying water, by tubes or otherwise, from the Ohio river, through the streets, lanes and alleys, and commons of the town of Cincinnati, for the purpose of supplying the inhabitants of said town therewith; which privilege may and shall be enjoyed by the said Company, their heirs, successors, and assigns, exclusively as aforesaid, for the term of ninety-nine years, from and after the passing of this ordinance, on the following terms:

1st. The said Company shall complete the work so far as to convey the water into that part of the town lying south of Third-street, commonly called the bottom, within two years from and after the first day of July next; and they shall convey the water into that part of the town lying north of Third-street, commonly called the hill, so as that the same may be delivered three feet above the first floor of James Ferguson's kitchen in the second ward of said town, within the term of three years from and after the said first day of July.

2d. After the said period of three years, the Company, their heirs, successors and assigns, shall continue to supply the citizens of the town, (or such of them as may desire to receive and pay for the same) with a sufficient quantity of water, making proper allowances for unavoidable accidents, and for the necessary repairing and renewing of their works.

3d. They shall permit water to be taken freely and without expense from their reservoirs and conductors, wherever the same shall be necessary to extinguish fires in the town, and for this purpose they shall provide for each square or block to which they conduct the water, a fire plug, or pen stock; and if the town Council shall at any time see proper to make reservoirs to be used in cases of fire, they shall be permitted to fill such reservoirs, free of expense, from the conductors of the Company; <u>Provided</u>, The said reservoirs be kept tight and in repair, and the water therein be used exclusively for the purpose of extinguishing fires.

4th. The Company, their heirs, successors and assigns, shall pay to the Town Council, yearly, and every year, during the continuance of the privileges herein granted, the sum of one hundred dollars, which payment shall commence one year after the works are completed. The money so to be paid shall constitute a free fund, and shall be appropriated under the directions of the Town Council, in such manner as they shall see proper, in providing and preserving such articles as may be useful in extinguishing fires.

5th. The said Company, their heirs, successors and assigns, shall be permitted to dig in the streets, lanes, alleys and commons of the town, for the purpose of sinking their conductors and of repairing them as often as may be necessary, leaving the surface of the street as before, causing as little inconvenience to the citizens as the nature of the case will admit: and they shall be permitted to demand and receive yearly, from the persons who shall use the water from their conductors, such sums as they may voluntarily agree to pay for the same.

6th. The privileges granted by this ordinance shall not be forfeited by a temporary interruption in the supply of water, occasioned by accident or the want of repairs in the machinery, reservoirs, conductors, or other parts of the works. <u>Provided,</u> such accidents be remedied, and such repairs be made within a reasonable time.

7th. During the term of ninety-nine years, herein before specified, no other person, or company, shall be permitted to convey water through the streets, lanes, alleys, or commons of the town, by tubes or other conductors, for the purpose of supplying the citizens of the town with water.

Sec. 2. <u>Be it further ordained,</u> That if the charter of the said Cincinnati Manufacturing Company shall expire, or the said Company be dissolved before the expiration of the aforesaid term of ninety-nine years, this ordinance and the privileges herein granted shall not thereby cease, but shall continue in full force and effect, and at the dissolution of the said Company, all the privileges herein granted shall vest in the persons composing the said company, at the time of such dissolution, their heirs and assigns, in the proportion of their several interests in the stock of the said company. <u>Provided,</u> The persons claiming the privilege aforesaid, comply with the terms herein before mentioned.

DONE by the Town Council of the Town of Cincinnati, at their Council Chamber, the 31st day of March, 1817.

WILLIAM CORRY, <u>Mayor</u>

Attest -- SAMUEL PERRY, <u>Clerk.</u>

ANTISLAVERY CONTROVERSY, 1836

Cincinnati was in a crucial geographical position very near the slave states. The controversies arising as a result of the abolitionist movement were bound to come to Ohio. The consequent struggles are exemplified in this early exchange over the right to express diverse viewpoints on the same issue. The selections chosen from this antislavery publication indicate some of the tactics used by both sides in the struggle.

Source: Executive Committee of the Ohio Anti-Slavery Society. <u>Narrative of the Late Riotous Proceedings Against the Liberty of the Press, in Cincinnati with Remarks and Historical Notices Relating to Emancipation</u>, Cincinnati, 1836.

ANTI-ABOLITION MEETING.

At a very large and respectable meeting of the citizens of Cincinnati, convened at the Lower Market House, in pursuance of a public call, on the 23d day of July, 1836, the following proceedings took place --
WILLIAM BURKE was elected President, MORGAN NEVILLE Vice President, and TIMOTHY WALKER Secretary.
The following preamble and resolutions were then unanimously adopted.
<u>Whereas,</u> The citizens of Cincinnati are now laboring under a serious excitement, in consequence of the existence of an Abolition Press in this city, from the influence of which, the most deplorable results may be justly apprehended. <u>And whereas,</u> While we recognize the constitutional right of liberty of speech and of the press, in its utmost extent; yet, being anxious to preserve the peace and tranquility of our city, and continue those amicable relations which have hitherto existed between the States, we deem it our duty to utter a warning voice to those concerned in the promulgation of abolition doctrines, through the aforesaid press, because we believe their course calculated to influence to passions of one portion of our yet unhappy country against the other, and to lessen that moral influence upon which the perpetuity of our Union mainly depend. Be it therefore
<u>Resolved,</u> That the spirit exhibited by the immediate supporters of the abolition press in this city, is entirely at variance with the feelings and opinions of the great mass of our population, is as unjust to our sister states, as it is prejudicial to our own quiet and prosperity.
<u>Resolved,</u> That the establishment of the said abolition press in this city is in direct violation of the solemn pledge heretofore given by its conductor at a public meeting on this subject.

<u>Resolved</u>, That in the opinion of this meeting nothing short of the absolute discontinuance of the publication of the said abolition paper in this city, can prevent a resort to violence, which may be as disastrous to its publisher and supporters, as it must be to the good order and fair fame of our city.

<u>Resolved</u>, That we will use all lawful means to discountenance and suppress every publication in this city which advocates the modern doctrines of abolitionism.

<u>Resolved</u>, That a committee consisting of twelve persons be appointed by the Chair to wait upon James G. Birney and his associates in the publication of the said paper, to remonstrate with them upon the dangerous tendency of the course they are pursuing, to communicate to them the actual tone of public feeling in the city, to request them by every motive of patriotism and philanthropy to desist from the publication of their paper; and to warn them that if they persist, we cannot hold ourselves responsible for the consequences.

The Chair then appointed the following persons as the above committee, viz: Jacob Burnet, Josiah Lawrence, Robert Buchanan, Nicholas Longworth, John C. Wright, Oliver M. Spencer, David Loring, David T. Disney, Thomas W. Bakewell, Stephen Burrows, John P. Foote, and William Greene.

To whom on motion the officers of this meeting were afterwards added.

It was then resolved that the committee publish the result of their interview, and that these proceedings be published in all the papers in the city.

The following resolution was then offered by Wilson N. Brown, and adopted.

<u>Resolved</u>, That we entertain the most profound respect for the memories of the venerated Patriots of more than "sixty years since" who in the harbor of Boston, <u>without</u> the sanction of law, but in the plenitude of the justness of their cause took the responsibility of <u>re-shipping</u> the Tea Cargo, and for which illegal act they were entitled to and did receive the warmest thanks and gratitude of every lover of good order and well-wisher of his country -- and that we in imitation of the noble and fearless example set us by those true-hearted Americans, declare that whenever we shall find an existing evil -- wicked and mischievous in its conceptions -- warring against the best interests and happiness of our common country by its effects -- aiming at the destruction and disunion of our happy government; and only prompted and sustained by those untiring engines of human ambition hope of gain and love of notoriety -- but shielded from legal enactment according to the usual practice of our laws so as to leave us but one channel through which we can rid our fair land from its withering influence, that in seizing that one tangible point our exertions shall be firm, and decided.

                              WILLIAM BURKE, President.
                              MORGAN NEVILLE, Vice President

TIMOTHY WALKER, Secretary

. . .The following resolution was adopted by the market House committee.

"Resolved, that the Executive Committee of the Ohio Anti-Slavery Society, be requested to communicate to the committee in writing, by 12 o'clock on Friday, to-morrow noon, an explicit answer to the question, whether they will discontinue or not the publication of an abolition paper in this city called the Philanthropist."

. . . Our Committee . . . agreed on the following reply to the request of the Market House Committee. It was handed in at the time mentioned in their resolution.

CINCINNATI, July 29, 1836.

J. BURNET, Ch. Com.

SIR: -- Whilst we feel ourselves constrained altogether to decline complying with your request, as submitted last evening, to discontinue the Philanthropist, we think it but just to ourselves, and respectful to our fellow citizens generally, to offer a brief expostion of the reasons that persuade us to this course.

1. We decline complying -- not so much from the fear that the particular cause in which our press in employed may be injured -- but because compliance involves a tame surrender of the FREEDOM OF THE PRESS -- THE RIGHT TO DISCUSS.

2. The Philanthropist is the acknowledged organ of some twelve thousand, or more, of our fellow citizens of Ohio, who believe that slavery, as it exists in our country, is altogether incompatible with the permanency of her institutions; who believe that the Slavery of the South or the Liberty of the North must cease to exist; and who intend to do, what in them lies, to bring about a happy and a peaceful termination of the former -- and this as speedily as facts, and arguments, and appeals to the consciences and understandings of the slave-holders can be made instrumental to effect it.

3. The Philanthropist is the only journal in this city or neighborhood, through which these facts, and arguments, and appeals can be fully addressed to the community. It has been conducted with fairness and moderation, as may be abundantly proved by the acknowledgements of those who are opposed to its objects. It has invited the slaveholders themselves to the use of its columns for the defence of slavery, and has given up to a republication of their arguments a large share of its space.

To discontinue such a paper under existing circumstances, would be a tacit submission to the exhorbitant demand of the South, that Slavery shall never more be mentioned among us. . . .

6. We decline complying -- because the demand is virtually the demand of slave-holders, who, having broken down all the safe-guards of liberty in their own States, in order that slavery may be perpetuated, are now, for the fuller attainment of the same object, making the demand of us to follow their example.

[The two remaining reasons were omitted -- unintentionally, we have no doubt -- in the published report of the Market House Committee. They were part of the letter sent to the Market House committee, and are here supplied.]

We decline complying -- because the attempt is now first made in our case, formally and deliberately to put down the freedom of speech and of the press. We are, to be sure, the object of the attack -- but there is not a freeman in the State whose rights are not invaded, in any assault which may be made on us, for refusing to succumb to an imperious demand to surrender our rights.

8. We believe, that a large portion of the people of Cincinnati are utterly opposed to the prostration of the liberty of the press -- and that there is among us -- whatever may be said to the contrary -- enough of correct and sober feeling to uphold the laws, if our public officers faithfully discharge their duty.

With these reasons -- to which many more might be added, did time permit -- we leave the case with you: -- expressing, however, our firm conviction, should any disturbance of the peace occur, that you, gentlemen, must be deeply, if not almost entirely, responsible for it, before the bar of sober and enlightened public opinion.

> JAMES C. LUDLOW,
> ISAAC COLBY,
> WM. DONALDSON,
> JAMES G. BIRNEY,
> THOS. MAYLIN,
> JOHN MELENDY,
> C. DONALDSON,
> GAMAL, BAILEY.

Executive Committee of the Ohio Anti-Slavery Society

J. BURNET, Chairman, &c. Cincinnati.

Thereupon, the following resolution was unanimously adopted by the Committee:

Resolved, That the members of this Committee reluctantly accepted the responsible trust committed to them, with no other motive than the hope of being able to allay the excitement which they believed to exist, and to prevent the violence which they feared might be its result. That, in discharging their duties, they have used all the measures of persuasion and conciliation in their power. That their exertions have not been successful, the above correspondence will show. It only remains, then, in pursuance of their instructions, to publish their proceedings and adjourn without day. But ere they do this, they owe it to themselves and those whom they represent, to express their utmost abhorrence of every thing like violence; and earnestly to implore their fellow citizens to abstain therefrom.

JACOB BURNET, DAVID T. DISNEY,
JOSIAH LAWRENCE, THOS. W. BAKEWELL,

ROB'T BUCHANAN.   JOHN P. FOOTE,
NICH'S LONGWORTH,   WILLIAM GREENE,
OLIVER M. SPENCER,   WILLIAM BURKE,
DAVID LORING,   MORGAN NEVILLE,
                TIMOTHY WALKER.

CITY PURCHASE OF WATER WORKS, MARCH 16, 1839

The city was authorized to purchase the water system in order to insure more effective operation of the works. This act was incorporated into the Charter of 1850.

Source: Cincinnati. <u>Charter, Amendments and General Ordinances of the City of Cincinnati.</u> Cincinnati. Revised 1850, pp. 73-74.

AN ACT authorizing the city of Cincinnati to purchase and conduct the city water-works.

142. SECTION I. <u>Be it enacted by the General Assembly of the State of Ohio,</u> That the city council of the city of Cincinnati shall be, and they are hereby authorized to purchase the property, rights and interests of the Cincinnati water company to the water-works; and for the purchase of said works, extending and improving the same, they are hereby authorized to create a debt not exceeding three hundred thousand dollars, to issue the bonds of the city therefor, bearing such interest as they may contract to pay, not exceeding six per cent. per annum, redeemable at such period as the said city council shall determine; to provide for the payment of the interest thereon, and for the final redemption of the debt, to pledge the property and revenues of the city therefor, in such manner and condition as may be necessary and proper to consummate the purchase of the works and negotiate the bonds.

143. Sec. II. And the city council shall have power to pass all ordinances that may be necessary to provide for the government, conducting and protection of the works, and the assessing and collecting the water rents, and in no case shall the rates of water rents be so low as not to ensure a net revenue of at least equal to the payment of the interest on the loan, and all other disbursements necessary for extending, repairing and conducting said water-works; and if in any year the rents should fall short of the necessary disbursements, the amount of such deficiency shall be levied and collected in the succeeding year in addition to the usual rents: <u>Provided,</u> that this act shall not become a law until it is accepted by a majority of the votes given, yea or nay, by the qualified voters of the city of Cincinnati, at an election to be held for that purpose at the usual place of holding elections, at such time as the city council of said city may direct, by giving public notice thereof at least twenty days previous to the holding of such election.

Passed March 16th, 1839.

CINCINNATI IN 1840

This description in The Cincinnati Almanac of 1840 indicates the pride with which its citizens held their city and the fact that the potential for growth and participation in trade was great. The fact that Cincinnati had grown with few public improvements was indicated as of great importance. In addition, the proposed construction of roads and canals would serve to give the city a connection with many areas of the Midwest.

Source: The Cincinnati Almanac, 1840. Cincinnati, 1840.

It is to be borne in mind that, Cincinnati has attained its present population, commerce, and manufactures, without the aid of any works of internal improvement but that of the Miami Canal, and to McAdamized turnpikes, one running 16 miles towards Columbus, and the other 12 miles towards Lebanon. Let us now see what improvements of this kind are actually in progress, the completion of which will directly and powerfully aid in the growth of Cincinnati.

1. The extension of the Miami Canal from Dayton to the Maumee Bay, which is already completed to Pequa 18 miles and is under contract, and in course of construction nearly to St. Mary's. A large portion of the residue to Fort Defiance is under contract. . . . The country on the borders of the upper part of the canal is fast filling up with an industrious people, and will soon yield a surplus of grain and pork for exportation.

2. A McAdamized turnpike from Chillicothe to Cincinnati, one third of which is constructed, and nearly all under contract.

3. The continuation of the Cincinnati, Columbus, and Wooster, and the Cincinnati, Lebanon, and Springfield Turnpikes, portions of which have already been constructed.

4. The Cincinnati and Harrison Turnpike, leading to the boundary line between Ohio and Indiana, a distance of 20 miles, which will be continued to Brookville, Indiana.

5. A McAdamized Turnpike from Covington to Georgetown and Lexington, Ky., which is now constructing, and about one third of it completed. The great importance of this road is but imperfectly appreciated by our citizens. It will lead into the heart of Kentucky, and will open new sources of trade and travel with the wealthiest part of that state.

6. The White Water Canal, the construction of which is wholly under contract, and a large portion completed, from the sources of White Water to Lawrenceburg, was in a line between Ohio and Indiana into the county of Hamilton, and thence branching to this city. . . .

7. The extension of the Cumberland Road through Ohio and Indiana, crossing the Miami Canal and the routes of several of the turnpikes already enumerated as they diverge from the north to this City.

8. The Little Miami Railroad running from this place up the valley of the Little Miami, and branching at Todd's fork, one track passing on to Xenia, and connecting with the Mad-River and Sandusky Railroad, . . . at Springfield, and the other stretching north-eastwardly to Columbus, and thence to Lake Erie, and Cleveland. . . .

9. The Cincinnati and Springfield Turnpike, 80 miles long, which will connect this city with the National Road. . . .

10. The improvements in the Licking River, which will extend navigation to West Liberty, Ky., a distance of 231 miles, at the foot of the mountains, where are large masses of coal, iron ore, extensive beds of limestone, sandstone, slate, lime, and marble; also white oak timber, hogs, cattle, and an almost inexhaustible supply of wood for fuel. The erection of thirteen locks for slack water navigation is contemplated and the work is under contract to be completed in 1840.

Fully to comprehend the influence upon which these various works will exert upon Cincinnati, it should be borne in mind that this city is near the centre of the largest and most fertile grain-growing region in the world, comprising more than 10,000,000 acres of land, and having within itself the capabilities of sustaining 4,000,000 inhabitants; that this rich and salubrious region is traversed by the Ohio, Licking, and Great and Little Miami Rivers, all of them navigable to some extent, and the two last eminently adapted to manufacturing purposes. . . .

Thus far the physical causes that are supposed to be operative in building up this city, have been principally considered. -- There are others that should not be overlooked. By recurring to the habits, tastes, and moral and intellectual culture of the population of the city of Cincinnati -- the number of their literary, scientific, and benevolent institutions -- their industry and enterprise -- their quiet and orderly observance of the laws and municipal regulations -- it will be found that these important elements in the progress and permanent prosperity of a city are strong, varied, and in active operation.

We cannot close this article without commending the taste and architectural skill that have been put in requisition in the construction of both our public and private buildings, within the last few years. . . .

Finally, it may be said that Cincinnati yields to no city in the Union in the inducements which she presents to a residence within the noble amphitheatre of hills that surrounds her. This is true in regard to the intelligence and refinement of society, the necessaries, comforts, and luxuries of life; the moral and religious character of her population: it is true in regard to the field which she presents for industry and enterprise in commerce and manufacture; it is true in regard to the opportunities she presents to the capitalist for safe and profitable investments in <u>real estate</u>.

REGULATIONS FOR GAS LIGHTING, June 16, 1841

As Cincinnati grew it began to face many problems and solve them with the best methods at its disposal. The development of gas lighting was recognized as a valuable aid to the city. James F. Conover, his heirs and associates were granted the right to install the necessary equipment to provide gas to the city. Provision was made that after the expiration of the twenty-five year charter, the city would have the right to purchase the gas works.

Source: <u>Digest of the Laws and Ordinances of Cincinnati, of a General Nature, Now in Force</u>. "Gas Lights." Cincinnati, 1842, pp. 82-84.

GAS LIGHTS.

An ordinance to provide for lighting the city of Cincinnati with Gas.

1. Sec. I. <u>Be it ordained by the city council of the city of Cincinnati</u>, That James F. Conover, his associates, their heirs, assigns, and successors, shall be and they are hereby vested with the full and exclusive privilege of using the streets, lanes, commons and alleys of said city of Cincinnati, in the State of Ohio, for the purpose of conveying Gas to the said city and citizens thereof, for the term of twenty-five years from the date hereof, and thereafter until the same shall be purchased by the city council of Cincinnati as hereinafter provided, and shall have full and exclusive power and authority to open and use the streets, lanes, commons, and alleys of said city, for the introduction of pipes and other apparatus for Gas: <u>Provided,</u> That the passage of the streets, lanes, commons and alleys is repaired to the satisfaction of the city council within a reasonable time, <u>and provided, also</u>, that the said streets, lanes, commons and alleys are not at any time unnecessarily obstructed.

2. Sec. II. That in consideration of the privileges hereby granted to the said Conover, his associates, their heirs and assigns, and successors, they, the said Conover, his associates, their heirs, assigns, or successors, shall furnish to the city, on the several streets, lanes, commons, and alleys, in which the leading or main pipes for supplying the citizens with Gas light shall be laid and in use, such quantity of Gas as may be required by the city council for public lamps at two-thirds of the lowest average price at which Gas shall or may be furnished to private individuals in the cities of New Orleans, Baltimore, New York, Louisville and Pittsburgh;

the lamp posts, connecting pipes, meters and lamps being furnished by and at the expense of the said city.

3. Sec. III. That said Conover, his associates, their heirs and assigns, and successors, shall, bona fide, commence the said Gas Works, and expend thereon the sum of $2000 within six months from this date, and shall have laid within two years from the date of this ordinance, six thousand feet of leading pipe for gas; and shall lay annually afterwards four thousand feet of leading pipe for gas, until the principal parts of the city shall be furnished with pipes. And if the city council should be desirous of erecting lamps at the Engine Houses, or other public buildings or bridges belonging to the city, and the said Conover, his associates, their heirs, assigns or successors should refuse, for a reasonable compensation, to extend the gas pipes to such situation or part of the city, the city council shall then have the privilege of extending the same, and provide such number of lamps for the purposes aforesaid, as they may deem necessary; and the said lamps shall be furnished with gas by the said Conover, his associates, their heirs, assigns or successors, at a price not to exceed two-thirds of the lowest average price at which gas shall or may be furnished to private individuals as aforesaid; and the said lamps shall be subject to the same regulations as other public gas lamps; and the gas pipes laid down at the expense of the city shall not directly or indirectly be used for furnishing gas to the individual citizens, nor shall other gas pipes be laid down within the portions of the streets, lanes, commons, and alleys occupied by the pipes of the city, until the whole amount expended for laying down the same be refunded by the said Conover, his associates, their heirs, assigns or successors.

4. Sec. IV. That the said Conover, his associates, their heirs assigns and successors, may, for all wilful and intentional injuries done by individuals to their fixtures, or apparatus, recover at law from such individuals doing said damage or injury, double the amount necessary to repair the damage or injury so done, to be recovered as other debts of like amount.

5. Sec. V. That the privileges hereby granted shall not be forfeited by any temporary failures on the part of the said Conover, his associates, their heirs, assigns or successors, to perform any of the conditions from them exacted, (except as to the commencement of the said works,) where such failures are occasioned by accident, untoward events, or the want of necessary repairs in the machinery or apparatus of said Gas Works: <u>Provided</u>, such accidents and events be remedied, and such repairs made within a reasonable time.

6. Sec. VI. That at any time after the expiration of the said twenty-five years, the said city council shall have the right and privilege of purchasing from the said Conover, his associates, their heirs, assigns or successors, their pipes, buildings, fixtures and other apparatus, owned and used by them in and about providing the city and citizens with gas, at a fair price and compensation. And the said price and compensation shall be ascertained and determined by five disinterested persons, two of whom shall

be selected by the city council, and two by the said Conover, his associates, their heirs, assigns or successors, and the fifth by the four thus selected or chosen.

7. Sec. VII. That all ordinances and part of ordinances heretofore passed by the said city council on the subject of Gas, are hereby repealed and annulled; and all privileges heretofore conferred by said council, inconsistent or incompatible with those conferred by this ordinance, are hereby rescinded and revoked.

Passed June 16th, 1841.

RECOMMENDATIONS FOR IMPROVEMENT OF NAVIGATION AROUND THE FALLS OF THE OHIO RIVER, 1846

The Ohio River was of primary importance to the commerce and industry of Cincinnati. This was indicated in the earlier document on the beginning of packet service on the river. The citizens were not going to sit by idly, but proceeded to recommend improvements in the locks so that river traffic would be improved. The selection indicates the concern of proposals of this group.

Source: <u>Proceedings of a Meeting of the Citizens of Cincinnati Held at the Council Chamber, January 22, 1846, Expressing the Sense of the Citizens on the Subject of Improving the Navigation Around the Falls of the Ohio River</u>. Cincinnati, 1846.

REPORT

The Committee appointed to report Resolutions for the consideration of the meeting respectfully state --

That the Citizens of Cincinnati, in common with the inhabitants of the Valley of the Mississippi, are deeply interested in the navigation of the Rivers of the Western Country; but more particularly in the commerce and trade of the Ohio and Mississippi, which form our principal channels of commercial intercourse with other portions of the United States, and with other sections of the world engaged in commerce.

The geographical position of our city being on the margin of the Ohio river, at the termination of several important lines of Rail Road, Turnpikes and Canals, conveying to this point the agricultural products of a very productive and fertile agricultural country, together with an extensive capital engaged in commerce, manufactures and steam boats, render our citizens easily affected in their business relations, by any improvement or interruption in the navigation of our principal Rivers.

The most important obstruction in the navigation of the western waters, occurs at the Falls of the Ohio, which are now passed by means of the Louisville and Portland Canal. To this work and the improvement of this part of the river we wish to call the attention of Congress, and, therefore, present the resolutions attached to this preamble. It is unnecessary here to describe the natural obstruction called the Falls of the Ohio, which are formed by a ledge or projection of a bed of Limestone Rock, entirely across the river, extending for one and a half miles, over which the river is increased in current and makes a fall of twenty-five feet, which renders this part of the stream impassable for steam boats, except during floods, which occur in the spring and fall. Before the Louisville and Portland Canal was completed, these rapids were avoided by a portage of two and a half miles, extending from Louisville to Shippingport. This portage and conveyance of produce and merchandize by land, on all kinds of vehicles, and over a bad road, when our commerce was but in its infancy, was then a very severe tax upon the shipper. As early as the year 1817 a few of the enterprising citizens of Cincinnati, to obviate the expenses and delay occasioned by a portage, attempted to contruct a canal around the falls on the Indiana side of the river; but for want of capital the work was abandoned, and the portage system continued. In 1825, the "Louisville and Portland Canal Company" was granted a very liberal charter by the State of Kentucky, in which the General Government participated, and commenced the construction of the present canal, which was finished in 1831. In 1836, a favorable survey by a competent engineer, for a spacious canal around the falls on the Indiana side, was authorized by individual enterprise; but the subject of a free canal to be furnished by the government being then agitated, further operations were suspended.

The imperfections of the Louisville and Portland Canal cannot be better illustrated than by quoting from the memorial of the citizens of Cincinnati, presented to Congress in 1844.

"This work which was intended as a facility to commerce and a benefit to the people of the west, has signally failed in accomplishing the purpose for which it was constructed; and as the government of the United States, with the benificent view of patronizing a work of public utility, became a partner in this canal, it cannot be thought invidious to call the attention of Congress to its deficiencies. . . .

. . . We offer the following resolutions:

Resolved, That the Louisville and Portland Canal around the Falls of the Ohio River, has signally failed in affording to the commerce of the Ohio such facilities as have been justly required by the public; and that the unfavorable location, and imperfection of the whole work could not be rendered suitable to the present trade, without incurring a greater expense, than a spacious canal would cost, located under more favorable natural advantages.

Resolved, That the People of the Mississippi Valley, have experienced great wrong from the participation of the general government as a principal stockholder of the "Louisville and Portland Canal Company," in imposing a ruinous tax for the last fourteen years upon the commerce of the Ohio river.

Resolved, That the rapid accumulation of steam boats, and the increase of commerce on the Ohio river, require another passage around the Falls of the Ohio, of sufficient dimensions to accommodate the largest class of Boats.

Resolved, That the Ohio river, for the purposes of navigation, being a national highway under the control of the general government, and not under the jurisdiction of the States bordering on it, the nation is bound to remove this important obstruction to the navigation of the river.

<u>Resolved</u>, That the citizens of Cincinnati, engaged in commerce, solemnly protest against any alteration of the Louisville and Portland Canal, which would interrupt the passage of steam boats, and cause a portage around the falls; as such an interruption would derange the whole business of the country, and be attended with incalculable losses and expenses.

It would also be highly impolitic, in the present warlike aspect of our foreign relations, to cause delay in the mail service, or to prevent the passage of war vessels, and such military and naval armament, as would be necessarily required from the manufacturing districts above this obstruction.

           GEORGE GRAHAM, Chairman.
           HENRY STARR,
           NATHAN GUILFORD,
           R.M.W. TAYLOR,
           CHAS. G. SPRINGER.

REVISED CITY CHARTER, 1850

The state legislature approved the revised city charter in 1850. This was done on the basis of the new state constitution, which provided for the general incorporation of all cities. The following selection indicates the manner in which all towns were to be governed. It is a consolidation of various acts passed previously.

Source: <u>Charter, Amendments, and General Ordinances of the City of Cincinnati.</u> Cincinnati, Revised 1850.

AN ACT to incorporate and establish the city of Cincinnati, and for revising and repealing all laws and parts of laws heretofore enacted on that subject.

1. SECTION I. <u>Be it enacted by the General Assembly of the State of Ohio,</u> That so much of the county of Hamilton as is contained within the following bounds, to wit: beginning on the Ohio river, at the east corner of fractional section number twelve, and running west with the township line of Cincinnati to Mill creek, thence down Mill creek with its meanders to the Ohio river, thence eastwardly up said river, with the southern boundary of the state of Ohio, to the place of beginning, shall be, and hereby is declared to be a city, and the inhabitants thereof are created a body corporate and politic, with perpetual succession, by the name and style of "THE CITY OF CINCINNATI," and as such, by that name, shall be capable in law of contracting, and being contracted with, of suing and being sued, pleading and being impleaded, answering and being answered unto, in all courts and places and in all matters whatsover; and also of purchasing, using, occupying, enjoying and conveying real and personal estate; and may have and use a corporate seal, and change, alter and renew the same at pleasure; and shall be competent to have, exercise and enjoy all the rights, immunities, powers and privileges, and be subject to all the duties and obligations incumbent upon and appertaining to a municipal corporation; and, for the better ordering and governing said city, the exercise of the corporate powers of the same, hereby and herein granted, and the administration of its fiscal, prudential and municipal concerns, with the conduct, direction, and government thereof, shall be vested in one principal officer, to be styled the Mayor; a board of trustees, consisting of three members from each ward, to be denominated the City Council, together with such other officers as are hereinafter mentioned and provided for.

2. Sec. II. That the said city of Cincinnati shall be and hereby is invested as the lawful owner and proprietor, with all the real and personal

estate, and all the rights and privileges thereof, together with all the property, funds and revenues, and all money, debts, accounts, and demands, due and owing, or in any wise belonging to said city, or which, by or under the authority of any former act or acts, have been acquired, vested in, or is, or may be owning or belonging to the city of Cincinnati, and the same are hereby transferred to the corporate body, created and established by this act; and all suits pending, and judgments recovered by, in favor of, or against said city of Cincinnati, together with all rights, interests, claims and demands in favor of, and against the same, may be continued, prosecuted, defended and collected in the same manner as though this act had never been passed.

3. Sec. III. The said city shall be divided into wards, as the boundaries thereof are now established, until such boundaries may be altered, or the number of wards may be increased by the city council, who are hereby authorized and empowered to make alterations in the boundaries of, or to establish additional wards, as the public convenience may require.

4. Sec. IV. That the mayor of said city shall be elected by the qualified voters thereof, on the first Monday of April, biennially, and shall hold his office for the term of two years, and until his successor shall be chosen and qualified. It shall be his duty to be vigilant and active at all times, in causing the laws and ordinances of said city to be put in force and duly executed; to inspect the conduct of all subordinate officers in the government thereof, and as far as is in his power to cause all negligence, carelessness, and positive violation of duty to be prosecuted and promptly punished; he shall keep the seal of said city, sign all commissions, licenses and permits which may be granted by or under the authority of the city council, and shall keep an office in some convenient place in said city, to be provided by the city council: he shall perform such duties and exercise such powers as from time to time may devolve upon him by the ordinances of said city, not inconsistent with the provisions of this act, and the character and dignity of his office, and generally do and perform all such other duties and exercise such other powers as pertain to the office of mayor; he shall, in his judicial capacity have exclusive original jurisdiction of all cases, for the violation of the ordinances of said city, and criminal jurisdiction in all cases where, by the laws of this state, justices of the peace within the township of Cincinnati, are or shall be authorized to hear and determine, or in any manner have power to act; and for the due and efficient exercise of the power herein and hereby vested in him, he shall have power, and it shall be lawful for him to award all such process, and issue all such writs as may be necessary to enforce the due administration of right justice throughout said city, and for the lawful exercise of his jurisdiction agreeably to the usages and principles of law: Provided, that in all cases brought before said mayor, for violations of the ordinances of said city, and when the said mayor shall adjudge the defendant or defendants to pay a fine of ten dollars or upwards, exclusive of costs, the defendant or defendants shall have the right of appealing from the said judgment to the

court of common pleas of Hamilton county, upon giving bond in double the amount of said judgment and costs, and with such securities as shall be approved of by said mayor, within ten days from the rendition of said judgment, which bond shall be conditioned to pay and discharge the judgment and costs which may be recovered against him, her, or them in the said court of common pleas, which appeal when perfected, by giving bond as aforesaid, shall entitle the party appealing to the same rights and privileges, subject to the same conditions, restrictions and limitations as by the laws of this state pertain to the parties appealing from the judgment of justices of the peace to the courts of common pleas; and the said causes so appealed shall be prosecuted in said court of common pleas by indictment and trial by jury, in the same manner as offences against the laws of the state are prosecuted, and it shall be sufficient to set forth in the indictment, the offence in the words of the ordinance said to be violated, and to refer to said ordinance by title only without reciting such ordinance, and by concluding the said indictment against the peace and dignity of the state of Ohio. And the said court of common pleas of Hamilton county, is hereby authorized, empowered, and directed to take cognizance of, and hear and determine all such cases as shall be brought before them by appeal as aforesaid, and to assess such fine, and pass such judgment against the defendant or defendants, as shall be prescribed by the ordinances of the city. The mayor shall moreover have authority to take and certify the acknowledgments of all deeds for the conveyance or incumbrance of real estates situated in the state of Ohio; and it shall be lawful for him to order any person brought before him charged with the commission of any criminal offence in any state or territory of the United States, upon proof by him adjudged sufficient, to direct such accused person to be delivered to some suitable person or persons to be conveyed to the proper jurisdiction for trial.

CITY CHARTER, NOVEMBER 2, 1926

The adoption of this new charter was a milestone in the government of Cincinnati and also set an example for municipal administration in many United States cities. The people chose to accept the proposals of their elected officials in permitting the development of the city manager form of government. The charter provided for the cooperation of the various branches of government and to permit the development of a more efficient system of administration.

Source: <u>Charter (adopted 1926) and Code of Ordinances (Revised June 28, 1928) of the City of Cincinnati</u>. Cincinnati, 1928.

CHARTER OF THE CITY OF CINCINNATI

Adopted by Vote of the People, November 2, 1926

We, the people of the city of Cincinnati, Ohio, in order to secure home rule, do adopt the following as the charter of our city: . . .

Article IV. Executive and Administrative Service

Section 1. The council shall appoint a city manager who shall be the chief executive and administrative officer of the city. He shall be appointed solely on the basis of his executive and administrative qualifications and need not, when elected, be a resident of the city or state. No member of the council shall be chosen as city manager. The city manager shall be appointed for an indefinite term, as hereinafter provided. He shall be removable at any time at the pleasure of the council. If removed at any time after he has served six months, he may demand written charges and the right to be heard thereon at a public meeting of the council prior to the date on which his final removal shall take effect, but pending and during such hearing the council may suspend him from office. The action of the council in suspending or removing the city manager shall be final, it being the intention of this charter to vest all authority and fix all responsibility for any such suspension or removal in the council. The council may designate some other officer of the city to perform the duties of this city manager during his absence or disability. The city manager shall receive such compensation as may be fixed by the council.

Sec. 2. Neither the council nor any of its committees or members shall interfere in any way with the appointment or removal of any of the officers and employees in the administrative service. Except for the purpose of inquiry, the council and its members shall deal with that part of the administrative service for which the city manager is responsible, solely through the city manager.

Sec. 3. It shall be the duty of the city manager to act as chief conservator of the peace within the city; to supervise the administration of the affairs of the city, except as otherwise specifically provided in this charter; to see that the ordinances of the city and the laws of the state are enforced; to make all appointments and removals in the administrative and executive service except as otherwise provided in this charter; to make such recommendations to the council concerning the affairs of the city as may to him seem desirable; to keep the council advised of the financial condition and future needs of the city; to prepare and submit to the council the annual budget estimate; to prepare and submit to the council such reports as may be required by that body and to perform such other duties as may be prescribed by this charter or required of him by ordinance or resolution of the council. The city manager shall have the powers conferred by law upon boards of control. Except as otherwise provided in this charter, all other executive and administrative powers conferred by the laws of the state upon any municipal official shall be exercised by the city manager or persons designated by him.

Sec. 4. The city manager, and such other officers of the city as may be designated by vote of the council, shall be entitled to seats in the council. None of said officials shall have a vote in the council, but the city manager shall have the right to discuss any matter coming before the council, and the other officers shall be entitled to discuss any matter before the council relating to their respective departments and offices.

Sec. 5. The city manager shall appoint a city solicitor. No person shall be eligible to the office who is not an attorney at law, duly admitted to practice in this state. He shall serve the council, officers and boards of the city as legal counsel and attorney, and shall represent the city in all proceedings in court. He shall act as prosecuting attorney in the municipal court. He shall perform all other duties now or hereafter imposed upon city solicitors by the laws of the state, unless otherwise provided by ordinance of the council, and such other duties as the council may impose upon him consistent with his office. The solicitor shall appoint his assistants and fix their salaries, but the maximum number of assistants and the total amounts of the assistants' salaries shall be fixed by council. The assistants shall hold their offices at the pleasure of the solicitor.

Sec. 6. The city manager shall appoint a city treasurer. The treasurer shall perform the duties imposed upon city treasurers by the law of the state of Ohio, except as otherwise provided by ordinance.

Sec. 7. The city manager shall appoint a director of public utilities. Except as otherwise provided by ordinance of the council, the director shall succeed to the powers and duties of the director of street railroads and the director of motor buses, and shall exercise the administrative powers of the city in relation to public utilities, except the Cincinnati water works, The Cincinnati Southern Railway, and any other municipally owned or operated utilities. The council shall refer to the city manager all applications and matters of proposed grants and renewals of grants for any public utility within the city. The city manager shall cause the director of public utilities promptly to investigate the same and the city manager shall report in writing to the council his advice and recommendations. The director shall perform such other duties as may be imposed upon him by the council or the city manager.

Sec. 8. The city auditor elected in the year 1923 shall not be subject to removal during the term for which he was elected except in accordance with the laws of the state. Thereafter, the city auditor shall be appointed by the mayor for a term of two years commencing on the first day of January in each even numbered year, and shall serve until his successor is appointed and qualified. Vacancies shall be filled in the same manner for unexpired terms. The city auditor shall be the chief fiscal officer of the city. He shall exercise supervision over all accounts, and accounts shall be kept showing the financial transactions of all departments of the city upon forms prescribed by him and approved by the city manager and the council. He shall submit to the city manager and to the council at its second meeting in each month a summary statement of revenues and expenses for the preceding month, detailed as to appropriations and funds in such manner as to show the exact financial condition of the city and of each department, division and office thereof. He shall perform the duties imposed upon city auditors by the laws of the state of Ohio, and such other duties as may be imposed upon him by ordinances of the council, but nothing shall prevent the council from transferring to other officers matters now in charge of the city auditor which do not relate directly to the finances of the city. He shall prepare and submit to the city manager such information as shall be required by the city manager for the preparation of an annual budget. He shall appoint his subordinates.

Sec. 9. The city manager shall appoint the superintendent of water works, who shall have charge of the administration of the Cincinnati water works. A sufficient charge shall be made for the supply of water, or any other public utility service operated by the city, to pay the expenses of such water works or other utility, the interest, sinking fund and retirement charges on bonds issued for such water works or other public utility, and for such improvements to said water works or other public utility as council may determine should be paid for without the issue of bonds. The city shall have the power to sell water outside of the city limits and outside of the state at such price as the council may determine. Revenue derived from the water works of the city shall be used for the purpose of said water works, and for no other purpose, and shall not be subject to transfer to any other fund. . . .

FIRST CITY MANAGER'S REPORT, January 5, 1927

> This report is of great importance to Cincinnati because of the confidence expressed in the new city manager form of government. The introduction of this new type of municipal administration was of great advantage to the city. Colonel Clarence O. Sherrill indicated that the city agencies had proven themselves to be quite amenable to working with his new office.

Source: <u>A Summary of City Manager Sherrill's Annual Report Before the Charter Committee,</u> January 5, 1927.

The Council City Manager form of government has been in operation in Cincinnati for one year, and under the sponsorship of the Charter Committee we are gathered here tonight to take stock and report the accomplishments, for the past year, of the business corporation known as the City Government.

It is with reluctance and almost embarrassment that I appear here before you on the invitation of the Charter Committee to describe some of the outstanding results accomplished by the City Administration; and in the recital that follows, I wish you would always keep in mind that the credit for all that has been done rests entirely with the nine members of the Council, exactly as any failure to accomplish would be charged to them. They are the direct representatives of the people, and accordingly, are responsible to the people for accomplishments and deficiencies. It is only through the whole-hearted interest and full co-operation of the members of the Council that the various departments can do effective work.

The Council, individually and collectively, has worked for the passage of legislation and has established policies having in view more efficient operation of City Government and the advancement of the City's best interests. They have improved, in many ways, the administrative organization of the departments, and have provided funds and legislative authority for many constructive improvements, and have provided for the proper functioning of all the departments of the City.

Among the more important pieces of legislation affecting the administrative departments was the revision of the Charter, passed by the Council and approved by vote of the people; the reorganization of the old Department of Public Works and its division into separate departments known as the Highway Department and the Sewer Department, placing under the Engineer of Highways all problems of construction, maintenance, and repair relating to streets and highways; and under the Engineer of Sewers all problems relating to the construction, maintenance, repair, and operation of sewers.

Another important piece of legislation that will have a great effect on the Building Commissioner's office was the authorization of a new Building Code, now in course of preparation by a voluntary citizen's committee.

A new Market Ordinance was passed of far-reaching effect and making possible a splendid development of the market system of the City under the Superintendent of Public Property. There have been numerous constructive pieces of legislation providing for construction programs in relation to the highways and sewers. The relations between the various committees of Council and the City Manager have at all times been most cordial, and they have given the strongest possible support and backing in all efforts made to improve conditions under the City Government.

Next to Council, I wish to give full credit to the heads of all the various departments and all of the personnel under them for their loyal and earnest efforts to give the maximum of service to the City. I wish here to pay tribute to the loyalty with which all my associates in the departments, from the chief officials down to the individual laborers, have served the public to the best of their ability in their respective jobs. . . .

THE SPIRIT OF THE NEW CINCINNATI, May, 1928

>This special edition of the Cincinnati <u>Enquirer</u> indicates the pride the populace had in their city. The development of industry, commerce, education, and various aspects of real estate are analyzed in order to emphasize the fine manner in which the city had grown.

Source: "The Spirit of the New Cincinnati," The Cincinnati <u>Enquirer</u>, May, 1928.

Industry, Commerce

Industry and commerce in Cincinnati are diversified and prosperous. The metropolitan district supports important branches of 103 of the 333 basic industries of the United States. These industries are represented by 3,025 manufacturing firms, employing 112,000 persons to whom an annual aggregate wage of $1,000,000,000 is paid. There are approximately 186,000 persons gainfully employed in Cincinnati.

Cincinnati leads the world in the production of soap, machine tools, playing cards, radio receiving sets and parts and in the manufacture of cigar boxes. The city's five largest industries annually produce goods of a total value of $265,000,000 divided as follows: Soap, $100,000,000; metal products, $60,000,000; clothing, $40,000,000; meat packing, $35,000,000; printing and publishing, $30,000,000. Cincinnati is the location also of several of the largest plants in the United States manufacturing office furniture, woodworking machinery, engineering appliances, laundry machinery, printing inks, boots, women's shoes, brushes, chemicals, pottery, safes and cabinets, and automobile parts. . . .

Arts, Science, Religion, Professions

The intellectual, spiritual, and physical welfare of the citizens of Cincinnati are advanced by institutions of the highest type and greatest progressiveness. The University of Cincinnati is one of the largest and best equipped municipal universities in the world. Its scholastic requirements are high, and it offers thorough education in all arts, sciences and professions. St. Xavier College is another notable seat of learning in Cincinnati, and is one of the foremost Catholic universities in the country.

Cincinnati's public school system, from kindergarten to high school, is nationally noted. The City has six public day high schools and two night schools -- the night schools now are rated as scholastically equal to the day schools -- three junior high schools, and three parochial high schools. The school system included 54 elementary schools, 13 colony schools, eight special schools, 10 vocational schools and 70 parochial institutions.

In addition, Cincinnati has 27 schools of music, 15 academies and preparatory schools, eight seminaries, eight business schools, several technical and industrial schools and institutions teaching oratory and dramatic art. The Cincinnati Art Academy is nationally known, as is the Art Museum, and the work done by the art colony here is of high merit. Two schools of music, the College and the Conservatory, are among the best in America. The medical, dental, law and engineering colleges of the University are especially fine. Ohio Mechanics Institute stands high among the institutions of its kind. Three large religious colleges -- Hebrew Union College, St. Mary's of the West and Lane Theological Seminary -- are also located at Cincinnati.

Other institutions fostering the culture of the city are the Public Library and its many branches and the Cincinnati Zoological Gardens. A bond issue has been approved for the erection of a magnificent new Central Public Library. In addition to its fine collection of natural life, the Zoo offers opera, concerts and other entertainment of the highest cultural order.

The spiritual needs of Cincinnati are ministered to by 403 churches. . . These churches work together with an encouraging degree of harmony and tolerance. One evidence of this spirit is the annual Community Chest campaign, when all denominations join hands in the interest of general charity.

The Cincinnati General Hospital is one of the finest and largest municipal hospitals in the United States. It was built with the future in view, and has justified the foresight of its creators. Among the city's great hospitals are such notable institutions as Christ Hospital, Good Samaritan, Bethesda and Deaconess. The Children's Hospital is the most modern of its kind in the country. In addition, Cincinnati is served by almost numberless smaller private hospitals. All of these institutions, great or small, are staffed by physicians and surgeons noted in their various specialities.

Real Estate, the Home, Building

Seven hills overlook the City of Cincinnati. The business section of the City is located on an extensive plain on the north bank of the Ohio River. Back of this plain on a sweeping curve, rises a chain of hills of great natural beauty. On these hilltops and the higher levels beyond are located the magnificent residential suburbs for which Cincinnati is famous

Cincinnati is a city of homes and of home-loving people. The crests and sweeping slopes of its encircling hills offer home sites picturesque and perfect. The tendency toward suburban residential life, and away from older and more congested districts, grew with the development of the automobile. This movement is now stimulated by excellent motor-coach service and other facilities for rapid public transportation.

Approximately 30 percent of the homes of Cincinnati are owned by the families that live in them. At the present rate of building more than 2,500 families annually are being provided with new homes. . . .

REPORT ON THE CITIZEN'S CHARTER COMMITTEE,
September, 1934

A group of concerned citizens of Cincinnati, during the 1920s, were determined to develop a system by which the affairs of their city would not be affected by concerns of the political parties. As a result the City Charter Committee was formed after adoption of the new city charter in 1926. The selections from the report of the National Municipal League indicate the methods used to organize the elections for better city government. Murray Seasongood, a former mayor or Cincinnati and president of the National Municipal League, added some of his own views to the report.

Source: Report of the Committee on Citizens Charter Organization of the National Municipal League. <u>The Cincinnati Plan of Citizen Organization for Political Activity</u>. New York, 1934.

CONDITIONS RESULTING IN ORGANIZATION OF CITY CHARTER COMMITTEE

In Cincinnati and Hamilton County before 1925 there were 6800 jobs and 683 precincts. This was an average of ten jobs to each precinct. If each job-holder could control two and a half votes in addition to his own, it meant 23,800 votes in the primary for the party in control of the jobs, and in the forty years preceding 1925, there was no primary election in which that block of votes was insufficient to control the nominations. After the nominations were secured in the primary, the ordinary voter had no choice of candidates. He had a choice between two hand-picked slates, the one termed Republican and the other Democratic.

In 1923 political conditions in Cincinnati were intolerable. The streets were impassable, the police and fire departments were undermanned. The city revenues were inadequate but the public had so completely lost confidence in their elected officials that extra tax levies and bond issues were consistently defeated at the polls. But one peculiar fact demanded explanation. This fact was that while a majority voted to elect officials nominated and supported by the old political machine it regularly voted with equal consistency or inconsistency to refuse adequate supplies of money to these elected officials.

In 1924, as a result of study of the situation, it became evident that the first steps necessary to correct the abuses of the political organization were to centralize responsibility and to require the voter to know at least the names of the candidates. Centralizing responsibility was proposed by cutting the number of councilmen from thirty-two, twenty-six of whom were elected by wards, to nine elected at large. It was proposed to accomplish the second objective by abolishing the use of party emblems upon the official ballots -- the eagle and the rooster in Ohio -- in municipal elections. A rallying cry was adopted, "Vote for men and not for birds," and the little group was named the Birdless Ballot League. The machine poked a lot of fun at the name "Birdless Ballot" and this was all to its advantage, as it centered attention on the movement. There were already in existence many groups of citizens that had each a particular panacea for all the ills to which the body politic was heir. Each was so convinced of the value of its own particular nostrum that it had refused to cooperate with any other group, and the political organization had fattened upon this lack of unity among its opponents.

Several of these groups were attracted to the ideas of the Birdless Ballot League. Its program fixed such a limited objective that it did not conflict with their own pet theories, and it might be made to work in harmony with their own plans. Groups that never before had cooperated with one another were willing to cooperate with it and came before it with their program. A group interested in the city manager form of government was in existence and the program of the Birdless Ballot League was finally extended to include a city manager. To avoid introducing controversial questions at the first election an amendment was drafted that changed but one section of the charter. It substituted for a mayor and a council of thirty-two elected largely by wards, a council of nine elected at large by proportional representation, and a city manager, selected by the council. To provide for the additional changes which were necessary, and to avoid controversial disputes at the first election, it was provided that six months after the first council elected under the amendment had taken office, it should appoint a commmssion of three to draft a complete revision of the charter and submit it to the electors.

Work was started to get over to the people the idea proposed and for that purpose a campaign of education was instituted. This was easy as there was no election of any particular candidates, and the question under discussion was the relative advantage of a different system of government. Appeals were made to mothers' clubs, church groups, men's and women's clubs, in fact to every group that had any interest in social ethics. The opportunity was always asked to have both sides of the question presented and to have speakers present who would represent the opposition. This resulted in frequent debates and a number of the best known leaders of the organization discovered to their astonishment that some of the impractical reformers were more convincing debaters than they, and that usually the audience was with the reformers and against the well known political leaders.

A woman was selected who had formerly been a secretary of the League of Women Voters to organize the women, and she was called the educational secretary. The results were surprising. Having learned the importance of the governmental change, the women were willing to help persuade their neighbors to vote for the amendment, and in a short time were working as precinct captains and block workers, calling on their neighbors, polling their precincts, and delivering campaign literature.

Nineteen hundred twenty-four was a presidential year and the LaFollette feeling was running high in Ohio. It was constantly insisted that the local question had nothing to do with national politics, but everyone was worried when the local Republican organization argued that the attempt to remove party emblems from municipal elections was an attack upon the two-party system. However, when the votes were counted it was found that the amendment had carried 92,511 to 41,105, that the two amendments to the city charter presented by the organization to confuse the votes had been defeated, and that the voters had separated national from local issues by giving Coolidge 95,000 votes, Davis 26,000, and LaFollette 31,000.

There was great enthusiasm over the victory and this was capitalized by giving a "victory dinner" at one of the large hotels. Nearly a thousand enthusiasts attended and many were turned away because the hall was too small. At that dinner a motion was made that the temporary organization be made permanent, and that preparations be made to take an active part in the first election under the charter. This was the beginning of the City Charter Committee.

FRAMEWORK OF CITY CHARTER COMMITTEE

Since that date the City Charter Committee of Cincinnati has conducted five councilmanic elections. In 1925, the first election under the new charter, six Charter councilmen, consisting of two Democrats and four independent Republicans were elected, while the Republican organization elected only three councilmen, although in the preceding election it had secured the mayor and thirty-one out of thirty-two councilmen. In 1927 the Charter Committee elected six councilmen consisting of two Democrats and four independent Republicans, while the Republican organization elected only two, an independent being the ninth. In 1929 the Charter Committee again elected six councilmen out of the nine, this time consisting of three Democrats and three independent Republicans. In 1931 the Charter Committee elected five councilmen -- three independent Republicans and two Democrats. The Republican organization elected four, one of whom was a negro who received almost the solid vote of his race. As everyone remembers, 1931 was a year in which opposition to those in power was reflected in election returns almost universally. In 1933 the Charter Committee again was successful in electing a majority of the council, of whom three were Democrats and two were independent Republicans.

This citizen movement and the government it inaugurated, have become so intimately a part of the everyday life and thought and conversation of

Cincinnatians, that a much broader meaning to the word "charter" has developed. There has passed into common usage a curious figure of speech by which the word "charter" is applied indiscriminately to persons, measures, and activities of the Charter Committee and the present government.

How was this change from organization Repbulican control to citizen control brought about? It was done by forming a ward and precinct organization and entrusting its control to a group interested in using the mechanism to benefit the citizens and not to serve selfish purposes. This was accomplished by adopting for political purposes the same sort of association that has proved successful in other community work. A chamber of commerce or a community chest consists of many persons who are interested in the performance of certain public work. No one is sufficiently interested to do the work alone, but all are interested enough to contribute money, work, or influence to the common cause. An unpaid board of directors is elected and this board selects competent, full-time, paid executives. The City Charter Committee adopted this plan. It utilized an unpaid board of directors and paid skilled executives. It aroused a new loyalty in the citizens by declaring that the responsibility rested upon them, and that all workers in the wards and precincts must be volunteers and must work for the cause of good government without any sort of personal remuneration for that work, for the system of party patronage would not be used to reward workers. The people of the city met the test and proved conclusively that the ordinary citizen is sufficiently interested in politics to give time, money, and work to the cause of bettering municipal government provided he feels that his work is accomplishing something and that he is not subject to the suspicion of making personal profit. . . .

The organization of the City Charter Committee was based upon the belief that the citizens in general were interested in politics and would be willing to do the detail work of politics if they could be made to feel that results could be secured. The City Charter Committee has stood six tests and believes it has a right to say that its method of organization has been tried and is worthy of being used as a model. After the first councilmanic election in 1925, the opponents of the Charter group said that the victory was an accident and that no reform administration ever succeeded itself. In 1927 these opponents explained the second Charter success by saying that the individual councilmen had done well and that the public had re-elected them, but that the real test would come when the attempt was made to elect new men. In 1929 this contingency was met. Seven new men ran on the City Charter ticket and the results were the same as in 1925 and 1927 -- the election of two thirds of the council. In 1931 and in 1933 the City Charter Committee elected five of its candidates. This demonstrated that the public is indeed interested in politics, and that men and women will work for the cause of good government without demanding the loaves and fishes of political patronage, and it showed that it is possible to secure volunteer workers and that these volunteer workers are much more effective than are paid professional workers.

The board of directors, the officers, and all members of committees, including all members of the ward and precinct organization, both men and women, are volunteers. No city employees are numbered among the workers of the City Charter Committee. All employees of the city are forbidden by the charter, by civil service laws, and by administrative rules to engage in political activity or donate money to any political organization. This is one of the vital elements of success in the maintenance of a citizen's municipal party.

In 1926, when the first city manager took control, every employee in the city was a worker in the Republican machine and had endeavored in every way to defeat the City Charter candidates. Many of the supporters of the City Charter Committee urged the wholesale dismissal of these employees and the appointment of Charter sympathizers and workers in their place. The decision was made to retain all of the old employees until proved unfit, to fill all vacancies in the administration from the civil service lists, and to forbid any political activity by employees of the city. This decision placed the responsibility for politcal work upon the interested citizens and took away the temptation to shift this work on to job-holders. Instead of mobilizing an army of city employees for political service, the existing army of political workers was demobilized.

The City Charter Committee has a rigid rule that no worker at the polls shall be paid for his or her service. Only the headquarters staff is paid; this principle is fundamental. In the organization of any municipal party, the temptation comes to pay workers at the polls in certain places where it seems to be very difficult to secure volunteers. If workers in any part of the city are once paid it become extremely difficult thereafter to obtain volunteer workers. Furthermore, volunteers of the type desired will not work if there is any possibility of the public misunderstanding their position and believing that they are paid. It was found to be much better to secure men and women as volunteers from other parts of the city who would go into the tought wards and serve as witnesses and challengers than to pay persons in these localities. In the first place, the man who must be hired to do political work is frequently susceptible to a bribe not to do the work for which he is paid. The tough ward and precincts of our city furnish interest and excitement for the younger men. In one of the elections a quota of witnesses and challengers, made up entirely of college men who had played football on college teams, was placed in the toughest ward in Cincinnati. The excitement and interest was so intense that every year, among the volunteer witnesses and challengers, there are men who insist that they be given a position in a tough ward.

The results have been astonunding. In 1923 four downtown wards -- the sixth, eighth, sixteenth, and eighteenth -- were the real controlling force in local politics, and the vote in the outlying residential wards was practically negligible. Since appointments have been made under civil service and city employees have been forbidden to do political work, the number of votes in the residence section has increased enormously, and the vote in the old machine wards has fallen off. Today in Cincinnati, charter people vote because they are interested in politics, not in jobs. The total vote in Cincinnati in 1929 was 135,000 against 123,000 in Cleveland, a city nearly twice as large.

This interest of the citizens in politics has not been confined to city affairs alone. Contrary to the predictions of the Republican machine that the national party would meet defeat locally if deprived of the service of city job-holders, President Hoover received in 1928 the largest vote ever cast in Hamilton County for a Republican presidential candidate. The fact that allegiance to the City Charter Committee in local elections has not weakened the ties of party loyalty on national issues is strikingly demonstrated by the fact that in a number of the wards in the Republican primary of 1928, City Charter precinct executives were elected to the Republican Central Committee and these executives openly owrked for the Republican ticket in the state and national election of 1928, and against the Republican machine in the city election of 1929.

Cincinnati has obtained material results. It has obtained clean and efficient government. Its streets are clean and in good repair. Its city hall has been cleaned outside and inside. It built more new streets and boulevards in the first six years than in the preceding twelve years. It has done all of this without increasing the tax rate and, in spite of the fact its net bonded indebtedness has been reduced by $4,522,543.82 which is a reduction of 10.7 per cent from December 31, 1925 to December 31, 1933. When many cities are experiencing difficulty in borrowing money and floating bond issues, Cincinnati's bonds are selling at a premium and at a low rate of interest, approximately 4 1/4% (January 1934).

Greater, however, than these material accomplishments has been the new spirit that has infused itself through the whole community. The young men now feel that they can take part in politics without compromising their own inherent sense of real values. The most serious injury that gang politics inflicts upon a community is the dulling of the idealism of young men. The graft of which the gang is the beneficiary after all affects the average citizen very little. It is the idea that in order to obtain political preferment it is necessary to ally oneself with the political gang, to close one's eyes to the combination between vice and politics, that gives a shock to the young man that permanently influences his character, and leads him to cynicism in regard to political life. . . .

STATEMENT BY MURRAY SEASONGOOD

Murray Seasongood, President of the National Municipal League and former Mayor of Cincinnati, had not become President and ex-officio member of the Committee when it drafted the foregoing report (publication of which has been delayed by lack of funds for printing). He contributes as an expression of his personal views the following additional thoughts:

1. The citizens' committee and no officer or member thereof should,

in any way, seek to dictate to or interfere with any city official. The attitude of the committee and its officers should be that if city officials request their views on any matter, they will give them but they will be scrupulously careful to avoid bossism or even the appearance of bossism through forcing their views on any of the city officials.

2. The citizens' committee must seek to obtain outstanding candidates having some large following or probability of getting a large vote. The essential is to get candidates who can be elected. It has been found that candidates who would make exceelent councilmen, if elected, cannot be elected because not sufficiently known. Organization is not enough. There are some persons in every community who can be elected without any organization support. Such persons, where suitable, should be included in the citizens' group list of candidates.

3. No person holding any official position in the city administration should be a member of the governing body of the citizens' group.

4. In experience, it has been found that certain persons who have been retained, in a desire for complete nonpartisanship, have been secretly working against the administration which retains them. Wherever there is a reasonable suspicion that such may be the case, the services of such person should not be retained if such person is not in the classified service.

5. Nomination and election are not enough. Between elections there should be constant education and notice of what is being done by the administration, given through bulletins, at large meetings, by radio, through the press, and otherwise. There should be a city club or other open forum for the discussion of local public matters where meetings are held weekly or at short intervals in order that objections, if any, to the administration may be publicly made and accusations refuted, if possible, in a public manner and in a way calculated to reach large numbers of persons. Otherwise, voters may become displeased over some fancied grievance and information attempted to be imparted within a month or two before election will not suffice.

THE MASTER PLAN, March 1946

Cincinnati had been more deeply involved in urban planning during a major part of the twentieth century than most other cities. After the Second World War great concern was evidenced about the directions to be taken by future planning commissions. This selection from the Master Plan of 1946 indicates the methods of approach as well as the aims of planning. All aspects were to be taken into account, including governmental services, transportation and business facilities, as well as regulations for the progress of the city.

Source: <u>The Master Plan.</u> Cincinnati, March 1946.

GOAL OF THE MASTER PLAN

The object of planning is not arbitrary control or regimentation of private initiative, but the co-ordination of all Area projects, public and private, to promote an orderly and balanced growth of the Area's framework and its separate parts in the best interests of all its inhabitants.

The Master Plan is a long-range program for meeting the present and emerging needs of the Area in a manner to make the most effective use of its economic and social resources. It is not intended as a static device. It should be kept constantly attuned to changing conditions so as generally to contain at all times such features as will be conducinve to the improvement of the Area, its future growth and development, and as will afford adequate facilities for the transportation, distribution, comfort, convenience, health and welfare of the population.

The studies of the Master Plan Division are therefore aimed at finding out what the wants of the people are likely to be in the future, what the Area will need to meet the competition of other areas, and to see in what ways and to what extent the Cincinnati Area can meet them.

Public Welfare is the Objective

Master planning is a technique or method for attaining an objective, and if the method be followed, the objective will result. Then what is the objective? It is the greatest attainable health, prosperity, safety, convenience and welfare of and for the present and future inhabitants of the city and its metropolitan area.

Skeptics sometime argue that master planners talk only about streets, buildings and other physical things instead of human beings. The viewpoint is wholly wrong. One might as well say that laboratory experiments seeking cures for cancer are concerned with test tubes and chemicals and other physical things instead of with human beings. It is the people who live and will live in the Area whose welfare is the object of master planning.

The social and economic welfare of the people is the objective of every social activity. What, then is the special objective of planning? It is to so arrange the physical plant, the lay-out of the Area, in which the population lives and works, that it will minister to and promote their social and economic welfare.

Uses of the Land Fundamental

Master planning is concerned with the future land use pattern of the city and the metropolitan area. We all live and work on the land or in buildings on the land. A street is a strip of land used for transportation. An apartment is a building on a piece of land. It is used for habitation. A school is a building on a piece of land. It is used for education. A city hall is a building on a piece of land. It is used for government. The whole Area is a collection of land uses.

Decide wisely upon the uses of the land and you decide wisely for the welfare of all the people.

A Problem of Distribution

How can those land uses so be distributed as to be productive of the greatest benefits to the population? That is the problem. It is important to note that we are dealing not merely with public land uses, like streets, playgrounds and public buildings. We are dealing equally with private land uses such as factories, stores and houses. The two are so interrelated that the public structures cannot be intelligently located without planning and regulating the nature and locations of the private developments.

It is this inter-relationship which makes master planning essential to economic and efficient community growth. If, for instance, the location of a street is determined without relationship to the locations of the homes and industries and shops, then the street will break down and blight, rather than build up and invigorate, the areas through and to which it runs, or the investment in the street will be more or less wasted. So we conclude that for the maximum attainable social and economic welfare of the people, the special distribution of the public and private uses of the land and territory must be studied and the program of development made up in accordance with the results of that study.

Time Plays Important Roles

The element of time also must be considered. Time plays two parts in the Area's welfare. In locating their places of habitation, gathering of food and other activities, animals think only for a short time ahead. Humans having, as we hope, the greater intelligence, know that they cannot get the best results without thinking a long time ahead. It is the special province of master planning to give predominant influence to long-term consideration.

Then, too, as we have only so much money to spend in any year, the program of development must be spread throughout the period of the Plan. To keep the whole Area's life in good balance, we should construct the buildings and projects in order of their urgency, measuring urgency in accordance with social and economic standards.

As all of this is important to everybody and paid for by everybody, all must participate. But just as a board of health is necessary to take the lead and organize the effort for the promotion of health, so an agency like a planning commission is necessary to take the lead and organize the planning.

Community Problems and Needs

All of these considerations were brought under scrutiny in determining the specific questions for which the Master Plan is to supply the answers. Some of the basic questions which arose at once are:

Can this Area continue to offer to people in all walks of life living conditions that are equal or superior to the best offered elsewhere? If not, what must be done to secure and hold leadership in that regard? Can it offer to its own young people and to progressive young people from other sections the opportunities for employment and advancement they seek? If not, what are its shortcomings and how can they be corrected?

Can this Area retain the manufacturing industries that it now holds, and can it attract others of appropriate types? If not, what steps are necessary to make it a better industrial location? Can it retain and strengthen its position as a commercial and cultural center? If not, what can it do to make its position stronger?

These are some of the fundamental community problems and needs to which the Master Planning Division must address itself, and, in due time, formulate proposals looking to their solution and satisfaction.

There are many more. For some of them the Master Plan will provide definite and conclusive recommendations, for others, it will at least point the way. For all of these the completion of the Plan is essential:

1. Protection of the residential neighborhoods against incipient blight.
2. Provision of good environment for and protection of future redevelopment and housing.
3. Strengthening and development of individual neighborhoods and communities for better living.
4. Reclamation of blighted areas, both residential and non-residential.
5. Park, open space and recreational requirements.

6. Public transit needs and relief of traffic congestion.
7. Transportation and terminal facilities -- rail, water, truck and air.
8. Flood control and river-front development.
9. Motorways system, including limited access expressways.
10. Traffic safety measures, such as grade-crossing eliminations.
11. Off-street parking facilities.
12. Conservation of the Central Business District.
13. Development of neighborhood shopping centers.
14. Provision for public markets.
15. Fire, police, health and other facilities.
16. Public utility requirements.
17. Locations of public and semi-public buildings.
18. Means of civic improvement and beautification.
19. Economic and industrial developments.
20. Labor supply and job opportunities.
21. Property assessment, taxation and revenue policies.
22. Comprehensive capital improvement program and budgeting.
23. Priority and necessity for public improvements.
24. Relation of the metropolitan governmenal units to the City of Cincinnati.
25. Regulation of perimeter development around the City.
26. Needed legislative enactments, local and state.

High Moral Qualities Required.

Building the future community in accordance with a master plan, one of the deepest and most vital of all techniques for social and economic betterment, calls not only for the application of intelligence on the part of every individual, but also for the exercise of high moral qualities.

Every one of us has special personal or private interests. It may be to the special interest of an individual that a factory does not go near his home. To another, that his business go where, from the standpoint of the welfare of all, a recreational area is more appropriate. Of course, the net aggregate of our special interests will, in the long run, coincide with the public interest. Nevertheless, some degree of conflict between the public interest and any individual's special interest at any given moment, is inevitable.

One of the highest of moral qualities is the capacity and the willingness to see that the long-run interest of all must be studied and permitted to have guiding influence. Alfred Bettman once said: "The future belongs to the city which plans for it. The quality of life in that future will be determined by the quality of that planning. The quality of that planning is the best evidence of the moral quality of the community."

REPORT ON RECREATION, December 1947

    Recognizing that recreational facilities were important for the redevelopment of the city, the City Planning Commission began to make a careful study of the existing and future needs of those areas required to offer all elements of the citizenry the proper facilities. The study included recommendations for expansion or addition of parks, playfields, and various special facilities. School playgrounds were also included in the study. Recommendations for various developments were carefully stated so that Cincinnati and Hamilton County could follow through with specific actions.

Source: Cincinnati. City Planning Commission. <u>Recreation: An Analysis of Its Administration and Program of Activities, and Facilities Required.</u> Cincinnati, December, 1947.

SUMMARY

    Recreation is now recognized as an invaluable adjunct to both education and character building. More and more it is acknowledged that recreational activities, in which a child is taught the important lessons of team play and social adjustment, are as important a part of education as are the three "R's."
    Recreation offers a constructive approach to a No. 1 problem -- juvenile delinquency. Overflowing penal institutions poignantly bespeak society's failure to cope with this question by punitive means.
    With these points in view, a recreation plan for Cincinnati's Metropolitan Area has been made. It is aimed at answering the need -- not only of youth -- but of older persons having leisure time. A well-rounded recreation plan hinges on the proper balance of recreational activities and the facilities necessary to accommodate them. This report deals with both of these important phases.
    Generally speaking, there are two main types of recreation: that which requires no supervision, and that which involves leadership and direction of groups of varying sizes and character. In the latter type, the programs may range from team sports and social or study activities to carefully planned and supervised activities for maladjusted individuals or groups.
    The biggest stumbling block to an adequate public recreation program in Cincinnati is lack of funds. As a result, this city's public program lags behind that of comparable cities. Programs and expenditures of private

agencies, however, surpass those of numerous other comparable cities. Whereas the Cincinnati Area has numerous facilities such as parks, playgrounds, picnic grounds, tennis courts and the like, a winter indoor program is lacking. Modern school buildings which can double as neighborhood recreation centers are still at a minimum, though the prospective building program will help to remedy this deficiency. There is much to be desired in the way of leadership, programs and facilities for smaller self-determining groups, and for individuals and groups needing psychological assistance to adjust themselves socially. Another outstanding need is for better programs for young adults.

Contributing factors to weaknesses in the public recreation program are the duplication of services and confusion of functions among the various public and voluntary agencies concerned with recreation. For instance, the Cincinnati Recreation Commmission, in stressing the acquisition and development of physical properties, has minimized the vital function of providing personnel for supervision of recreational activities. The city's program gives uneven geographical coverage and fails to provide all-year community centers.

The Park Board's recognized function of conserving and beautifying its properties has been consistently carried out. More adequate funds should be provided, however, and more recognition given to the needs of older people for nearby small park areas.

In connection with its current extensive site acquisition the building program, the Cincinnati Board of Education recognizes the broader recreational aspects of its school plants. Still to be determined, however, is its policy as to direct participation, as contrasted with cooperation, in recreational programs involving its properties. In any case, creation of a Youth Services Section in the school administration is recommended. . . .

There is an urgent need for better joint planning and action among the public and private agencies. Fuller participation in recreation matters by citizens is another prerequisite.

In appraising recreation areas and facilities within reach of Metropolitan Cincinnati, three general types are recognized. The first, regional recreation areas within 100 miles' driving distance of Cincinnati, appear to be adequate in prospect though not in fact today. Further appropriations must be obtained from Ohio and Indiana state legislatures, however, to finance construction of nine authorized park projects within 90 miles of Cincinnati. With completion of development, these areas -- parks, reservations, forests, conservancy areas, historic sites and quasi-public areas -- will be adequate to serve the Cincinnati area.

The second type consists of parks, playfields and special facilities within the metropolitan area that have widespread rather than merely local appeal. Existing metropolitan parks on upland sites within or close to urban development appear to be adequate to answer needs of the populace except in Campbell County, where a bluff park is proposed between Ft. Thomas and the cities on the river bench below. Additional county parks may be needed in the future in addition to the three now in process of development or acquisition. The lowlands are not generally well-adapted to or available for large parks, but do offer sites for summer camps, and for a few playfields of metropolitan character. Additional metropolitan playfields are proposed for development by expanding Walnut Hills and Western Hills playfields; by public acquisition of Twin Oaks Golf Club in Kenton County, and by creating a metropolitan river beach and adjacent land development around existing Tacoma Beach in Campbell County. Provision of some special recreational facilities, especially for boating, are proposed in conjunction with general re-development of the Cincinnati Central Riverfront. Other special facilities with wide drawing-power, especially ballfields, may be developed in conjunction with expressway rights-of-way, in order to be conveniently accessible, and along the river bench both up and down-stream.

The third type consists of recreation areas to serve the daily needs in residential communities and neighborhoods. Areas and facilities for all ages are needed: the playlot for very small children, where practicable; the playground for children of elementary school age; the playfield for teenagers and adults; special facilities such as swimming pools, baseball fields, miniature golf course, bowling greens, archery ranges, and recreation buildings, that may occur separately if not as features in playfields; local parks, for quiet play, and as resting-spots for the numerically-increasing older age-groups.

Few localities are now adequately equipped with such facilities. Blighted obsolete neighborhoods should acquire them in connection with redevelopment, with new suburban areas and as required amenities in conjunction with subdivision approval. Otherwise-good existing neighborhoods, to remain desirable, must correct present recreational deficiencies. Besides the Basin, Walnut Hills, Clifton Hills, Avondale, and East Price Hill are especially deficient in playgrounds and playfields in relation to their population.

A tentative Master Plan for Community and Neighborhood Recreation Facilities includes existing areas and proposed school grounds, supplemented by other play areas and local parks, designated where need is indicated. This plan must remain elastic and should be subjected to further detailed scrutiny.

RECOMMENDATIONS

B. In connection with <u>Metropolitan Recreation Areas and Facilities</u>:

1. That efforts be made to obtain funds for completion of development of Winton Woods, and for acquisition and development over a reasonable period of time of <u>Western Reservation</u> as a county park; and that acquisition and development of other tracts proposed by the Hamilton County Park District be deferred pending evidence of their need.

2. That in accordance with the Master Plan for redevelopment of the Cincinnati Central Riverfront, the immediate waterfront be developed as a park, with emphasis on provision for boating facilities and waterside promenade, and including a historical memorial section in the vicinity of Lytle Park to commemorate the original site of Ft. Washington and the early history of the Cincinnati Area.
3. That Walnut Hills and Western Hills playfields be enlarged, as proposed by the Recreation Commission, to the status of metropolitan playfields, and that a public golf course be developed in conjunction with Western Hills.
4. That consideration be given by the Hamilton County Park District to provision of group camp facilities in its areas, and by the Cincinnati Park Board, of additional day camps.
5. That an adequate system of public swimming pools be developed throughout the metropolitan area.
6. That serious consideration be given to the turning over of <u>Columbia Park</u> by the Cincinnati Board of Park Commissioners either to the Ohio Archeological and Historical Society or to the Hamilton County Park District.
7. That in connection with development of the expressway system, attention be given to acquisition of incidental areas for baseball fields, tennis courts, and other special recreation facilities.
8. That efforts be continued to secure passage of anti-stream pollution legislation, and after its passage, to speed effectuation in connection with rivers of the metropolitan area. . . .

C. In connection with <u>Community and Neighborhood Recreation Facilities</u>:

1. That 1 acre each of playground, playfield, and neighborhood park, or a total of 3 acres, for each 1,000 of population served, be regarded as a minimum standard for communities and neighborhoods in the Cincinnati Metropolitan Area.
2. That if at all possible a neighborhood playground comprising from 5 to 7 acres be provided in conjunction with every junior and senior high school.
3. That where present and proposed school playgrounds and playfields will be too remote to serve residential areas of considerable size, additional play areas be provided by the proper local agency.
4. That if possible, neighborhood parks be provided as integral parts of playgrounds and playfields, and where these give incomplete coverage of need, additional park areas be added.
5. That in connection with large-scale housing developments, planning commissions see to it that suitable provision is made for playgrounds and for playlots for very small children.
6. That no unneeded school sites or other public property be offered for sale in areas earmarked for future redevelopment, and that

pending redevelopment, consideration be given to use of such properties, or others which may be obtainable, for interim recreational use, with a minimum of expenditure for improvement.

THE METROPOLITAN MASTER PLAN,
Adopted November 22, 1948

The long period of involvement in the Second World War had further added to the delays in proper urban redevelopment. City planning, recognized since the 1920s as a necessity in order to maintain the primary position of many cities, was now of even greater importance. Cincinnati adopted its master plan for urban restoration with specific recommendations for relocation of industries and housing within the core city as well as expansion of mass transportation and highway facilities. The basic objectives of the plan are printed below as an indication of the aims of Cincinnati as well as the intentions of city planning in general.

Source: Cincinnati. City Planning Commission. <u>The Cincinnati Metropolitan Master Plan and the Official City Plan of the City of Cincinnati</u>. Cincinnati, November 22, 1948.

Broad Objectives of the Plan

Throughout the project the City Planning Commission has recognized promotion of the social and economic welfare of the people of the Area as the basic purpose of the Master Plan. Accordingly, it was developed with the chief ends in view of realizing the maximum potentialities of the Area in terms of the most satisfying and healthful living conditions and the highest degree of economic well-being attainable by its people.

Expansion Potentialities

As American cities go, Cincinnati is a mature community. The growth of the Metropolitan Area hs been relatively modest in recent times, averaging about 10 per cent per decade since 1900. In view of the rapid slowing down of population growth in the nation, Cincinnati along with most metropolitan cities is likely to grow still more slowly in the years ahead. Careful estimates based on population trends and economic potentialities indicate average population increases of about three per cent during each of the next three Census decades.

The prospect that the Metropolitan Area may experience only modest population increases in the future does not mean that there will not be considerable expansion of its area. The loosening up of older, congested sections; the continued outward trend of residential construction; the demands of industry for larger sites; the need of additional open spaces -- these along with some increase in population and a somewhat greater one in the number of households will combine to extend the limits of the urban area. An expansion of the urbanized portions of the Area to the extent of about 30 per cent in approximately 25 years is not unreasonable to expect.

Basic Planning Problems

The Area thus faces two great planning problems, (1) to provide for the orderly development of peripheral land and the normal processes of expansion, and (2) to restore and maintain the livability and attractiveness of the inner communities.

The two processes involved are to a large extent complementary. The forces of expansion and of aging are controllable. Sound urban planning must consider their mutual relationship and develop effective methods for their control.

Development on the Periphery

The expansion on the outskirts must be controlled to the full extent made possible by the governmental powers of the political subdivisions of the Area. Much has been done, particularly through the traditional co-operation in dealing with larger geographical entities between the Cincinnati City Planning Commission and the Hamilton County Regional Planning Commission established in 1929. Much more can be accomplished through efficient land subdivision, zoning, protection, more comprehensive building codes and standardized requirements for public utilities and services within streets.

In the absence of regulations, the desire for the advantages of "country" living, away from the noise, smoke, traffic and congestion of the city proper, tends to ignore proper safeguards as the outward trek continues. Those who move out look only to the present and wave aside the fact that sooner or later adequate public services will become a necessity and that their cost will be very great.

Shoddy building construction, poor land subdivision, absence of zoning protection, and other similar deficiencies in new areas of scattered development produce more and worse blighted areas. This result is inevitable unless measures are taken which will prevent repetition of the mistakes which produced the slums and the blighted areas, actual and potential, which now afflict the central city.

Since their establishment, the influence of the several planning commissions within the Area upon the protection of old and the development of new neighborhoods has been continuous and beneficial. The commissions must play an even more vital role in the future. They must use to a greater extent than heretofore their powers to require adequate planning of subdivisions, large and small, and to achieve their amalgamation into organized and balanced neighborhoods. Many small subdivisions in the past have made provision only for streets and building lots. Parks, shopping centers and other facilities for modern living have been conspicuously lacking.

Planning needs to play a more positive and constructive role in shaping future areas for living.

Restoration of Inner Communities

As for the older city, a major long-range objective of the city's planning program under the Master Plan is rehabilitation and redevelopment of declining areas, to hold and attract a balanced proportion of families of varied incomes and sound business and industry within the city limits. This is both a social and an economic necessity.

The Master Plan indicates the areas for which redevelopment (for residence or industry) or rehabilitation is proposed. Redevelopment involves complete clearance, replanning and rebuilding. Rehabilitation calls for a variety of treatments.

When and if state urban redevelopment legislation is passed, it will probably be the function of the planning commissions to designate specific areas as those needing redevelopment under the Master Plan; to prepare a land use plan for each redevelopment project with new and proper densities determined; and, in the effectuation of each project to apply appropriate zoning and planning controls.

In connection with rehabilitation areas, planning commissions will prepare plans for the physical improvement of each neighborhood involved. These plans will look to such physical changes or additions in streets, parks, playgrounds, schools and public utilities and services as are required to restore the specific neighborhood to attractive and more livable condition. Other public departments will apply programs related to health, sanitation, safety and the like. Repair of residences, education of owners and tenants and stimulation of neighborhood interest are the tasks of property owners, tenants and civic organizations.

All available ways and means must be exerted to conserve good residence neighborhoods. Action on the recommendation of the Cincinnati Committee to Expedite Housing for a separate housing code to provide minimum standards for existing dwellings with respect to conditions affecting health will go a long way in this regard. The retroactive features of such a code will give the building department adequate power to require buildings to be so maintained that neighboring property is not adversely affected. The Committee's recommendations for the adoption of comprehensive and objective methods for determining the quality of existing housing and the establishment of a program for the condemnation of substandard dwellings will make distinct contributions in the same direction if adopted and acted upon. . . .

Refashioning the Land Use Pattern

The first and perhaps the most essential process is the readjustment of the basic pattern over a period of years in order eventually to separate the urban producing and distributing machine from the living areas.

Underlying this approach is the proposition that cities have two primary functions: (1) to furnish healthful, convenient, safe and attractive areas for living, and (2) to provide other areas, which should possess comparable attributes, for making a living.

Between these two functions there is a natural conflict. The intrusion of factories into residential neighborhoods is of course undesirable, but so also is the encroachment of dwellings upon areas needed for industrial development.

For some years the very size of industrial establishments, the scale of activities they generate and the amount of traffic they attract have had a debilitating effect on nearby residential sections. The coming of the railroads, then the motor vehicle, and the tremendous increase in city traffic have had radical physical consequences for which Cincinnati has failed to make adequate provision and adjustment.

Many evidences of physical deterioration and unsatisfactory living conditions in Cincinnati as in other cities are traceable to this conflict between the city as a producing machine and the city as a place of residence. The effects of this conflict can be redressed only by planning appropriate locations for each function and by insulating one against the other.

The Plan is therefore directed toward making secure, and restoring where needed, the desirability and stability of residential communities and neighborhoods and the improvement of industrial and commercial areas.

In approaching this problem the Master Plan has followed three major lines of attack, (1) Organization of Residential Sections; (2) Consolidation of Industrial Areas, and (3) Functional Organization of Public Services.

Organization of Residential Sections

The plan for achieving improved living areas consists of the reorganization of existing residential sections and the development of new ones as individual communities, each more or less self-contained, and each further organized into neighborhoods. . . .

The chief purpose of the Plan for an integrated system of communities is to reintroduce in Cincinnati as a metropolitan center the advantages of the self-contained city of medium size. The concept of these communities will be clear if they are thought of as cities of about 20,000 to 40,000 population, self-contained in respect to the everyday life of their inhabitants except for such facilities and services as will continue to be located in or supplied by Cincinnati as the central city, and by institutions serving the Metropolitan Area.

By reproducing over a period of years in each of the communities which are to make up the whole of the Area, an approximation of the physical pattern of a medium size city, re-creation of some of the desirable environmental and social conditions characteristic of such cities will be promoted.

In this manner we can recapture the advantages of the medium size city in each of these communities and at the same time make available those institutions to be found only in a great metropolitan city, for example: the University, the Art Museum and the Symphony Orchestra -- things a town of even 100,000 population can rarely afford. We can then capitalize to the fullest extent all the advantages which urban society can offer the average family.

Fortunately, an excellent basis already exists for organizing the Metropolitan Area into communities and neighborhoods. The Area is made up of a number of natural residential communities with separate identities as social and civic units. Building on this foundation the Master Plan rounds out the system and reinforces it by introducing features that will maintain and strengthen the unity of these communities and by eliminating or avoiding features which would tend to interfere with or weaken it. The physical plan cannot, of course, create a community or a neighborhood but it can and will assist other forces in fostering a true community and neighborhood spirit.

Four basic forces are at work, or can be put to work, to bring about this objective:

1. The number and size of the communities in the Plan correspond fairly closely to our junior high school districts. A junior high school, along with several elementary schools, one for each neighborhood unit, constitutes perhaps the most potent force for community cohesion and solidarity. The Cincinnati Board of Education is now committed to the type of organization that divides grades on the 6-3-3 basis, that is, the first six grades in an elementary school, the next three in a junior high school, and the final three in a senior high school building. A junior high school requires at least 15,000 to 20,000 population from which to draw.

2. Another unifying feature in most of the communities is or will be a community business district, a secondary business district in relation to the Metropolitan Area as a whole, but the chief center of commercial activities so far as the community is concerned.

3. Wherever and whenever possible a "community civic center," bringing together in a group of unified composition such buildings as a branch library, a recreation center, a health center, a branch postoffice, and in some cases appropriate semi-public buildings, is a third force helping to establish and maintain the identity and cohesion of each community. The civic center will usually be combined with or adjoin the community business district.

4. The size of each community in point of both area and population is limited by physical features separating one from another. In addition to topographic features such as deep valleys, steep hillsides and the flood plains of streams, these "separators" consist of industrial belts, railroads, expressways and modified expressways, large parks and parkways, green belts of public and private open spaces, cemeteries and institutions, singly or in combinations. Each neighborhood, too, is demarcated by topography, green belts or thorofares, or sometimes only by the intangible barrier of tradition. . . .

<u>Consolidation of Industrial Areas</u>

The Master Plan provides for a further concentration than now exists of the Area's industrial machine into belts or corridors. These will contain most of the industries, railroad lines and other rail facilities and the trunkline motorways. These motorways, generally of expressway or modified expressway design, industrial parking areas, recreational open spaces or topographic features such as steep hillsides are among the elements employed in the Plan to buffer the living areas against those devoted to industry.

Consolidating in this fashion the Area's production and major transport facilities and separating them from residential neighborhoods is not as difficult in this Area as in some others.

The topography here intially limited the choice of locations for railroads and industries. By and large, both were forced to stay in the valleys notwithstanding the flood danger which was not removed to any great extent until very recently. The residential settlements, on the other hand, naturally sought the hilltops as soon as developments in transportation made this possible. Of course, conscious efforts beyond this natural evolution will be required to achieve the necessary separation of basic land uses. But with an already existing pattern of the sort which has grown through the years the task will be facilitated.

Within the separating corridors there will be brought about improved transportation by rail and highway, further flood protection and grading, the closing of unneeded streets to make possible the assembly of large parcels, and the gradual elimination of substandard residential uses characteristic of such areas. All of these operations, both public and private, are parts of the Master Plan program to fit these industrial areas better for the purposes they are to serve. (See chapter on Industrial Areas.)

Functional Organization of Public Services

The third major line of attack of the Master Plan is concerned with the provision of the many necessary or desirable kinds of metropolitan and community facilities and services, appropriately located and in scale with anticipated needs. Such facilities as those for shopping, health, education, recreation, circulation and transportation, and public services such as police and fire stations and the like, are included.

Where possible, facilities of governmental or cultural character are combined in a planned community civic center or in a building containing municipal offices. Commerical activities are concentrated in community, neighborhood and local shopping centers. . . .

CENTRAL BUSINESS DISTRICT CIRCULATION SYSTEM
January, 1957

> The problem of the core of the business center in Cincinnati with its mounting traffic difficulties was becoming even more serious as the 1950s progressed. In addition proposals have been growing for establishing pedestrian malls and reducing the amount of vehicular traffic. The selection from this report indicates some of the issues involved, and the methods to be used and questions answered in the study.

Source: City Planning Commission. <u>The Proposed Central Business District Circulation, January 1957.</u> Cincinnati, Ohio, 1957.

<u>The Nature of the Central Business District and Core</u>

The City, in its physio-economic sense, is the physical environment created by western civilization for facilitating the exchange of goods, of services, and of ideas. The Central Business District originated as that part of the City where the greatest number and rapidity of exchanges could be made.

These exchanges could be classified in many different ways for many different purposes, but for purposes of understanding the physical characteristics of the C.B.D. which are the province of City Planning, they were grouped into seven major functions:

        Manufacturing
        Retailing
        Wholesaling with stock
        Wholesaling without stock
        Business Services
        Consumer Services
        Residence

The relative importance of these functions has shifted and changed through the passing years, and those which are dominant today are the ones which can pay the highest price for <u>concentration</u> and for <u>accessibility.</u> Concentration and <u>accessibility</u> are the two virtues of the C.B.D. which cannot be duplicated <u>together</u>, and <u>to the same degree,</u> elsewhere in the city.

The greatest concentration exists within the Core of the C.B.D. It can be seen in the height of buildings. It can be measured by counting people. It is demonstrated by the intense overlapping of the three major functions: Retailing, Business Services, and Consumer Services. These are the three functions which draw the greatest numbers of people. The greater the concentration of people; the greater their dependence upon pedestrian accessibility and pedestrian circulation. This plan endeavors to facilitate pedestrian circulation where it is needed most . . . . in the Core.

There is no danger of the Core losing its relative importance or its geographical position in the forseeable future. All research studies provide evidence of stability within the Core. Some studies, such as those for property assessed values and the building permit values show increasing concentration taking place in the Core while the rest of the C.B.D. is decentralizing or holding its own. Space devoted to retailing is increasing in the Core while decreasing in the Frame.

The rest of the C.B.D. is no less important than the Core, but because of less concentration there is less difficulty of accessibility. In the Frame there is less dependence on pedestrian circulation and more dependence on vehicular circulation. The Core and the Frame of the C.B.D. are complementary to each other. Together they create the setting for the business center of Cincinnati.

THE CIRCULATION PLAN

The problems faced in trying to improve accessibility while maintaining or increasing concentration have been baffling for years because the one is the antithesis of the other. A clue to a solution is provided by the design of modern shopping centers. Modern shopping center design has been perfected to the extent that pedestrian circulation dominates the center of the center, frequently in a "mall" between stores. Stores surround the "mall" and parking is on the outside of the stores. Truck service is provided in a location separated from pedestrians and parking sometimes underground.

When endeavoring to apply those features to an existing business district, certain questions obviously emerge.

> How can we convert downtown streets into pedestrian malls when we need the streets for vehicular traffic?
>
> How can we reduce congestion and accommodate more people at the same time?
>
> How can we separate the several forms of circulation: trucks, cars, transit, and pedestrians without making them less effective or extravagantly expensive?

There is no perfect solution. An ideal solution would require complete separation of all forms of transportation and extensive redevelopment of every block in the C.B.D. This would be prohibitively expensive or extend the accomplishment over an inconceivably long period of time. It was considered more reasonable to develop a plan which could be accomplished within the foreseeable future and within the existing framework of streets and structures. This plan results in many compromises between ideal and practical solutions, but it will be possible to see accomplishments soon, and within the limitations that exist in Cincinnati.

It consists of two steps. The first step is to reduce the amount of vehicular traffic in the C.B.D. The second step is to follow a plan for integrating all forms of circulation in a system which will utilize each to its most effective capacity and will control each so as to least interfere with the others.

The plan proposed here depends upon converting the Core into an area which will be predominantly (though not entirely) for pedestrians. Some Core streets will be converted into pedestrian malls, or plazas, to create sections of the Core called "Pedestrian Preserves". The Core area will be penetrated by a series of loop streets which will carry traffic into the Core, but not through it. The penetration loop streets, with connecting service alleys, will provide places for trucking and other delivery services. Parking will be provided in locations outside of the Core, situated so as to intercept travel between the expressways and the Core. People leaving their cars will be carried to the Core on overhead pedestrian ways.

CINCINNATI ETHICAL CODE, DECEMBER, 1963

Municipal governments had become increasingly aware of, and concerned with, mismanagement and corruption. In particular many officials had become used to accepting gifts from people who were doing business with the city government. In addition, some members of the city staff had taken second jobs that sometimes called upon them to give certain information to which they were privy. As a result, the Cincinnati council established a code of ethics that provided specific regulations for all those employed by the city. This report, published in the New York Times, gives the basic aspects of the new code.

Source: "Cincinnati Aides Get Ethical Code; Curbs Imposed on Gifts and Outside Employment." New York Times, December 26, 1963, 44:1-2.

The 5,600 employes of the city of Cincinnati will be governed by a code of ethics, effective January 1.

The code, approved last week by William C. Wichman, City Manager, forbids outside employment that might directly or indirectly influence the performance of duties for the city and bars acceptance of valuable gifts from any company offered in connection with the performance of duty.

Violation of the code may constitute a cause for suspension or removal from office or job or "other disciplinary action" the code stipulates.

Each city employe will be given a card asking the question: "Do you have any outside employment?"

If the answer is "no," there will be no further questions. If the employe answers "yes," he will be required to fill out a form detailing the nature of the outside work and he can request permission to continue the latter.

If his request is denied, he can appeal to the Board of Ethics....

The code provides:

"No one shall use his official position for personal gain or shall engage in any business or transaction or shall have a financial or other interest, direct or indirect, which is in conflict with the proper discharge of his official duties."

Disclosures Barred

"No one shall, without proper legal authorization, disclose confidential information concerning the property, government or affairs of the city," the code says, "nor shall he use such information to advance the financial or other private interests of himself or others."

Referring to acceptance of gifts and favors, the code says:

"No one shall accept any valuable gift whether in the form of service, loan, . . . or promise from any person, firm or corporation which is interested directly or indirectly in any manner whatsoever, in business dealings with the city; nor shall anyone accept any gift, favor or thing of value that may tend to influence him in the discharge of his duties. . ."

Elaborating, it goes on:

"No city employe shall accept from any contractor or supplier doing business with the city, or wishing to do business with the city, any material or services for the private use of the city employe."

The code also prohibits employes from representing private interests "in any action or proceedings against the interest of the city in any matter in which the city is a part."

In regard to outside employment, the code says

"No one shall engage in or accept private employment or render services for private interests when employment or services are incompatible with the proper dischage of his official duties or would tend to impair his independent judgment or action in the performance of his official duties."

RIOT AFTER MARTIN LUTHER KING FUNERAL,
April 8, 1968

The deep sense of loss with which many blacks received the news of the death of Dr. Martin Luther King, Jr. was expressed in many memorial services on the day of his funeral. In some cases people were so angry that the slightest incident exploded into violence. Such was the case in the Avondale section of Cincinnati. This article from the Cincinnati Enquirer indicates how the riot broke out and how it was finally quieted down.

Source: Allen Howard, "Pride, Peace Go Up in Smoke of Hate," Cincinnati Enquirer, April 9, 1968, p. 36.

Pride, Peace Go Up In Smoke of Hate

The peace, quietness and the proudness shown at a memorial service for Dr. Martin Luther King, Jr. Monday afternoon went up in smoke about 30 minutes after the services were over.

Negro leaders found themselves helpless against a band of roving youths who smashed windows, set fires and looted a dozen businesses in Avondale before the riot act and a curfew were called about 7 p.m.

The memorial services were peaceful with Negro leaders calling for unity among black people. Rev. Harold Hunt, pastor of Carmel Presbyterian Church, called for Negroes to "forget any differences of the past and face the future with unity."

The tempo was stepped up when Mrs. Margaret Washington, president of the Welfare Rights Group praised Dr. King for his leadership in the field of civil rights.

A prelude to what was to come came in a speech by John Poole, vice-chairman of the Cincinnati Congress of Racial Equality. Poole received a loud ovation when he told the 1500 persons gathered at Avon Recreation Center, "The white man killed King, the best thing for us to do is to get the white man back. The way he has been getting us for all these years."

The meeting broke up, without a song, without an incident. Members of a newly created security force patroled the area as the crowd dispersed.

Barry Turner, president of the Avondale Community Council, the sponsoring group, called a press conference at the council headquarters, Reading Road and Mann Pl. The crowd moved in that direction, still orderly.

A Negro woman was shot accidently by her husband at Forest Avenue and Reading Road.

As she was carried off to the hospital, nearly 500 orderly persons in the block from Rockdale Avenue to Forest on Reading Road, changed into something else.

A pawn shop at Forest and Reading was looted and jewelry was discarded on the streets.

Clyde Vinegar, one of the organizers of the memorial service ran to a Negro policeman and told him that a group of Negroes were going to beat up a white policeman who had been sent to the area to help.

It became a contest among angry youths, Negro leaders and the police, black and white. Windows in a liquor store were smashed and liquor was stolen, bottles broken and strewn on the streets.

The youths smashed windows in the LoMark Discount Drugstore, Reading Road and Rockdale Avenue. They set fire to the store. The crowd moved toward the area with loud cheers as the flames mounted.

A Negro policeman was told to put away his shotgun that maybe the crowd would quiet down. As he put it in the trunk of his car, he was hit by a bottle.

Avondale became a bedlam of hate with roving youths moving into the Burnet and Rockdale area. They smashed the window in the Center Dry Goods Store. Small children, young girls and women, men in their early twenties began looting the store.

Cars pulled up in front of the store. The occupants got out, unlocked the trunk of their cars and loaded them full of clothes. Young kids, about eight or nine were seen putting stolen clothes under an apartment near Rockdale and Burnet Aves.

Rioting and looting moved south from Burnet. Youths hit Gerber Drugs, Big Louie's restaurant, a laundromat, a dry cleaners and Mike's Parkview Market. Again cars pulled up and loaded with groceries.

Another group moved south on Reading Road setting fire to Siegal Furniture Store, Windham Avenue and Reading Road. They smashed windows at Wolf's Barber Shop, Harry's Foods Store and Kyrk's Flower Shop.

As the riot squad moved into the area, they were jeered and heckled by roving teenagers. Members of the riot squad calmly told people on the streets "Move out of the area for your own safety. We are not playing. This is serious."

And it was.

ANTI-RIOT ORDINANCE, APRIL 17, 1968

As a result of the riots that occurred following the death of Martin Luther King, Jr. the city council and municipal officers found it necessary to increase the powers of the mayor and the city manager to act quickly during the times of crisis. The six Republican members of the council voted for the resolution, whereas the two Charterite and one Democratic members opposed this action. The mayor and city manager were given permission to act without first consulting the council. Provisions provided for informing the governor and sheriff as well as for proclamation of a state of emergency. Specific powers to limit activities and meetings were included in this act.

Source: Cincinnati. The City Bulletin. vol. XXXII, No. 18, April 30, 1968, pp. 4-6.

AN ORDINANCE No. 172-1968

Adopting supplementary Article XVIII of the Administrative Code entitled "Public Danger or Emergency" in order to better define and authorize the actions and procedures necessary to deal with man-made and natural disasters and emergencies.

Whereas, it is advisable to establish as part of the Administrative Code a clear statement of the powers of the various City officials and the procedures to be followed by them in times of riot or other public danger and emergency and

Whereas, the establishment of such procedures and authority is necessary in order to assure that during the time of public danger or emergency the law will be enforced firmly with justice and equality; now, therefore:

Be It Ordained by the Council of the City of Cincinnati, State of Ohio:

Section 1. That Article XVIII of the Administrative Code, entitled "Public Danger or Emergency" is hereby ordained to read as follows:

ARTICLE XVIII
Public Danger or Emergency

Sec. 1. Purpose. The purpose of this Chapter shall be to better define and authorize actions and procedures to be taken by the City Manager, the Mayor, and other officers of the City of Cincinnati in time of public danger or emergency. Nothing herein shall be interpreted as limiting the authority of the Mayor or City Manager to take any appropriate action in time of public danger or emergency which he is authorized to take under any other provision of the Code of Ordinances, the City Charter, the Statutes or Constitution of the State of Ohio, or the Laws and Constitution of the United States of America.

Sec. 2. Definitions.

A. "Public Danger or Emergency" shall mean:

1. A riot, as defined in any degree by the Ohio Revised Code, any civil disturbance, disorder, or other occurrence that constitutes a clear and present danger to the health, safety and property of the citizens of the City of Cincinnati, or substantially impairs the functioning of the City government and its ability to protect the lives and property of the people; or

2. Any natural disaster or man-made calamity, or clear and present danger thereof, including but not limited to flood, conflagration, cyclone, tornado, earthquake, or explosion within the corporate limits of the City of Cincinnati resulting in the death or injury of persons or the destruction of property to such an extent that extraordinary measures must be taken to protect the public peace, health, safety, or welfare.

B. "Absence" shall include incapacity of the Mayor, Vice-Mayor, or City Manager or inability to make immediate contact with the Mayor, Vice-Mayor, or City Manager.

Sec. 3. Duties of the City Manager. In time of public danger or emergency until the Mayor, or in his absence the Vice-Mayor, assumes the duties of commanding the police, maintaining order and enforcing the law under Section 1 of Article III of the City Manager shall perform such duties and shall immediately proceed to take all action necessary to preserve and protect the public peace and the lives, persons, and property within the City of Cincinnati that are endangered or potentially endangered by the factors constituting such public danger or emergency.

He shall establish and put into effect procedures whereby circumstances or events which constitute a public danger or emergency or which are likely to be productive of a public danger or emergency shall be immediately reported to him by members of the departments under his authority and control. Upon receipt of any information of circumstances or events which may constitute an actual or potential public danger or emergency, he shall immediately convey such information to the Mayor, or in the absence of the Mayor, to the Vice-Mayor. Thereafter, he shall convey such information to all other members of Council as soon as is practicable. He shall establish procedures to be used in his absence for so notifying the Mayor, the Vice-Mayor and the members of City Council. He shall continue in his efforts to contact the Mayor or Vice Mayor in accordance with the provisions of this Article even though he proceeds to act in their absence.

The City Manager shall establish procedures for taking positive action through all the appropriate departments of the city under his jurisdiction to control and suppress riots and to protect the public peace and the lives, persons and property within the City of Cincinnati in times of emergency and shall keep the Mayor informed in detail as to these plans and preparations. He shall consult with the Mayor in regard to the formulation of such plans and preparations for the purpose of providing a course of action that can be pursued effectively and expeditiously by the City under his direction or the direction of the Mayor. The City Manager and the Mayor shall keep the Vice-Mayor informed of all plans and procedures for dealing with public dangers or emergency, in preparation for the possibility of the Vice-Mayor assuming such duties in the absence of the Mayor. In the absence of the Mayor and the Vice-Mayor, he shall be authorized to proceed to take any action he deems necessary under the provisions of this Article and to exercise their powers as set forth herein. . . .

Sec. 5. Proclamation of Emergency. When the Mayor, or in his absence of both the Mayor and the Vice-Mayor, the City Manager determines that a public danger or emergency as defined in this article exists, he shall forthwith proclaim in writing the existence of the same and the time of its inception and shall issue proclamation thereof to the public through the news media and such other means of dissemination as he deems advisable.

Prior to issuance of the proclamation as provided for above and prior to assuming command of police as provided for in Section 6 of this Article, the Mayor, or in his absence the Vice-Mayor, shall, to the extent that time and the availability of the persons listed herein permit, confer and consult with the Safety Director, Police Chief, Fire Chief, Members of Council and other persons conversant with the circumstances that exist.

Sec. 6. Mayor May Assume Command. In time of public danger or emergency, as defined and proclaimed above, the Mayor, or in his absence the Vice-Mayor, is hereby authorized and given the consent of City Council to take command of the police, maintain order, and enforce the law under the provisions of Article III, Section 1 of the Charter of the City of Cincinnati and to do all things necessary or advisable in regard thereto. He may exercise any power or authority granted to mayors, administrative heads of cities or police chiefs by the laws of the State of Ohio.

Sec. 7. Emergency Orders. The City Manager, or the Mayor if he has assumed command as provided in Section 6 above, or the Vice-Mayor, if he has assumed command in the absence of the Mayor, may, as he deems advisable in the interest of the public peace, health, safety or welfare and in regard to the specific area or areas of the city imperiled by the public danger or emergency or the city as a whole, as he deems advisable, make and enforce orders to do any or all of the following:

A. Prohibit or limit the number of persons who may gather or congregate, or prescribe conditions under which such persons may gather or congregate, upon the public highways or public sidewalks or any outdoor place, or in any theater, restaurant, place of public assembly or commercial establishment to which the public has access;

B. Restrict or prohibit movement within, above, or beneath the area or areas which, in his judgment, are imperiled by the public danger or emergency;

C. Suspend operations at municipal airports;

D. Establish a curfew during such hours of the day or night as he deems advisable and prohibit persons from being out of doors during such curfew.

E. Prohibit or restrict the retail sale, distribution, or giving away of gasoline or other liquid flammable or conbustible products in any container other than the gasoline tank properly affixed to a motor vehicle.

F. Order the closing of gasoline stations and other establishments engaged in the retail sale, distribution or dispensing or giving away of liquid flammable or combustible products.

G. Prohibit or restrict the sale, distribution, dispensing or giving away of any fire-arms or ammunition of any character whatsoever.

H. Order the closing of any and all establishments or portions thereof engaged in the sale, distribution, dispensing or giving way of fire-arms and/or ammunition.

I. Prohibit or restrict the carrying or possession on the public streets or public sidewalks or in any public park or square or any other public place a weapon or any object intended to be used as a weapon including but not limited to fire-arms, bows and arrows, air rifles, sling shots, knives, razors, broken bottles, fire bombs, missiles or any kind, clubs, blackjacks, billies, chains or similar items.

J. Prohibit or restrict the retail sale, distribution, dispensing or giving away of acids, caustics, or any chemicals or other substances capable of being used singly or in combination to cause injury or damage to persons or property.

Sec. 8. Additional Assistance for Police and Fire Divisions. The City Manager is authorized to contact with other governmental agencies and firms and corporations providing security or fire services for the furnishing of additional police and fire protection during times of public danger or emergency. Such agreements may be reciprocal in nature.

Sec. 9. Duration of Emergency. The public danger or emergency proclaimed in accordance with above procedures shall exist until the officer declaring such emergency shall determine that the event or occurrences constituting the public danger or emergency no longer exists, provided that, such duration shall not extend beyond two weeks from the time of its proclamation unless extended by action of City Council, and further provided that City Council may, at any time it determines that the public danger or emergency no longer exists, declare it to be at an end.

Section. 10. Authorization of City Departments to Act. The various departments, divisions of the City of Cincinnati and the personnel thereof are hereby authorized to exercise whatever powers and authority are necessary in order to carry out the orders of the Mayor, the Vice-Mayor, or the City Manager issued in time of public danger or emergency as set forth in this Article.

BIBLIOGRAPHY

The works cited have been carefully selected to indicate the major sources to be consulted for further research on the growth and development of Cincinnati. Materials listed have been published during the nineteenth and twentieth centuries. A variety of works was chosen to provide a cross-section of the information on the social, economic, and political life of the city. Students should also consult Reader's Guide to Periodical Literature and Social Science and Humanities Index for further articles on Cincinnati.

PRIMARY SOURCES

Act Incorporating the City of Cincinnati and the Ordinances of Said City Now in Force. . . Cincinnati, 1828.

An Act Incorporating the City of Cincinnati, and a Digest of the Ordinances of Said City, of a General Nature, Now in Force. . . Cincinnati, 1833.

Administrative Code of the City of Cincinnati, 1956. Cincinnati, 1956.

Arnold, Bion J. Report on Interurban Electric Railway Terminal System for the City of Cincinnati. Submitted to the Cincinnati Urban Rapid Transit Commission. October, 1912.

Benzenberg, George H. Report to the Board of Trustees, "Commissioners of Waterworks" of Cincinnati, Ohio. A Brief History of the Old Waterworks, leading up to and including the Construction of the new Waterworks. . . Cincinnati, 1909.

Charter, Amendments, and General Ordinances of Cincinnati. Revised 1850. Cincinnati, 1850.

Charter (adopted 1926) and Code of Ordinances (revised June 28, 1928) of the City of Cincinnati. Cincinnati, 1936.

Charter and Ordinances (revised to January 1, 1936) of the City of Cincinnati. Cincinnati, 1936.

The Cincinnati Almanac for... 1839-1840 Being a Complete Picture of Cincinnati and Its Environs. Cincinnati, 1839-40.

Cincinnati. . . . Annual Message to Cincinnati Citizens from the City Manager. 1932-date

Cincinnati. Annual Reports of the City Departments. 1860/61-1861/62, 1863-1914. Ceased publication in 1914. It was superseded by the Cincinnati Yearbook.

Cincinnati. Annual Report of the City Manager. 1926-date.

Cincinnati. Chamber of Commerce. Annual Report. 1855-1862

Cincinnati. City Manager's Office. A Workable Program for Urban Renewal. Cincinnati, 1955

Cincinnati. City Manager's Office. Urban Redevelopment Division. An Urban Renewal Program for Cincinnati. Cincinnati, 1953.

Cincinnati. City Planning Commission. Airports in the Master Plan. June, 1946. Cincinnati, 1946.

Cincinnati. City Planning Commission. Central Business District Plan. Cincinnati, 1957. 2 vols.

Cincinnati. City Planning Commission. The Cincinnati Metropolitan Master Plan and the Official City Plan of the City of Cincinnati, adopted November 22, 1948. Cincinnati, 1948.

Cincinnati. City Planning Commission. Downtown Riverfront Development Plan. Metropolitan Master Plan. Cincinnati, 1946.

Cincinnati. City Planning Commission. Industrial Land Use, Present and Future. . . . Cincinnati, 1946.

Cincinnati. City Planning Commission. The Master Plan; Report on the Program and Progress. Cincinnati, 1946.

Cincinnati. City Planning Commission. Motor Way. Cincinnati, 1947.

Cincinnati. City Planning Commission. Parking: A Study of Present and Future Needs in Down Town Cincinnati. Cincinnati, 1947.

Cincinnati. City Planning Commission. Public Transit. Cincinnati, 1948.

Cincinnati. City Planning Commmission. Recreation: An Analysis of Its Administration and Program of Activities, and Facilities Required. Cincinnati, 1947.

BIBLIOGRAPHY

Cincinnati. City Planning Commission. Redevelopment of Blighted Areas. Cincinnati, 1951.

Cincinnati. Education Board. Proceedings, 1933-date.

The Cincinnati Enquirer. Centennial Edition. Cincinnati, 1963.

Cincinnati. House of Refuge. Annual Report. 1852-1894

Cincinnati. Mayor. Annual Messages, 1870-1933. Title from 1912-1921 and 1929-1930 was Annual Report. From 1933-date the Mayor's Annual Message is included in the City Bulletin.

Cincinnati. Metropolitan Housing Authority, Report. 1935-date

Cincinnati. Municipal Reference Bureau. The March of City Government, City of Cincinnati (1802-1936). Cincinnati, 1937.

Cincinnati, Ohio. Civil Service Commission. Rules and Regulations... March, 1912. Cincinnati, 1912.

Cincinnati, Ohio. Fire Department. Annual Report. 1853-date.

Cincinnati, Ohio. Public Works Department. Report on Plans and an Estimate of the Cost of a Rapid Transit Railway and an Interurban Railway Terminal for the City of Cincinnati, Ohio, December, 1914. Cincinnati, 1914.

Cincinnati, Ohio. Waterworks Department. Annual Report. 1847-date.

Cincinnati, Ohio. Waterworks Department. Rules and Regulations. Cincinnati, 1876.

Cincinnati Steam Boat Company. Articles of Association of the Cincinnati Steam Boat Company. Cincinnati, 1823.

Cincinnati Yearbook. The City Manager's Annual Report. 1926-date. 1926-1938 have title: Municipal Activities.

Cincinnati Zoning Board of Appeals. Annual Report. 1931-date.

The Cincinnatian. Official Organ of the Cincinnati Chamber of Commerce. December, 1913-1937. 1932-37, title: Cincinnati Chamber of Commerce News Bulletin. Ceased publication, 1937.

The City Bulletin; Official Publication of the City of Cincinnati. 1932-date.

Digest of the Laws and Ordinances of Cincinnati, of a General Nature, Now in Force. Cincinnati, 1842.

Digest of the Principal Ordinances of Cincinnati, Passed Since 1835, of a General Nature, Now in Force. Cincinnati, 1838.

Laws, Rules and Regulations for the Government of the House of Refuge. Cincinnati, 1861.

Memorial of the Citizens of Cincinnati, to the Congress of the United States, Relative to the Navigation of the Ohio and Mississippi Rivers.

Ohio Anti Slavery Society. Narrative of the Late Riotous Proceedings Against the Liberty of the Press in Cincinnati With Remarks and Historical Notices, Relating to the Emancipation. Cincinnati, 1836.

Ordinances, Rules and Regulations, Department of Water Works of the City of Cincinnati. Revised to July 1, 1944. Cincinnati, 1944.

Proceedings of a Meeting of the Citizens of Cincinnati, Held at the Council Chamber, January 22, 1846, Expressing the Sense of the Citizens on the Subject of Improving the Navigation Around the Falls of the Ohio River. Cincinnati, 1846.

Quinn, James A. Building Permits; Trends and Distribution, Cincinnati, Ohio, 1908-1938. Columbus, Ohio, 1941.

Reed, Ellery Francis. A Program for the Development of Public Welfare for Cincinnati. Cincinnati, 1927.

Scowden, T.R. Special Report on the Extension and Enlargement of the Cincinnati Water Works. Cincinnati, 1872.

Statutes Regulating the Civil Service of the City of Cincinnati. March 1, 1912. Cincinnati, 1912.

Sullivan, J.B. A Plan for Facilitating Rail Freight Movements in the Cincinnati Area. Cincinnati, 1947.

United States Works Progress Administration. Ohio. Natural Trades... Cincinnati, 1941.

SECONDARY SOURCES

Allen, Lee. The Cincinnati Reds. New York, 1948. A detailed study of the Cincinnati Reds from the time of their organization as amateurs in 1886 to the 1940s.

BIBLIOGRAPHY

Baker, Avis. . . . Cincinnati as a Western Outpost of Boston Liberalism. Chicago, 1918. Interesting analysis of the development of thought and how it spread.

Beckjord, Walter C. "The Queen City of the West" -- During 110 Years! A Century and 10 Years of Service by the Cincinnati Gas and Electric Company (1841-1951). New York, 1951.

Brasnam, Jim. Pennant Race. New York, 1952. Interesting analysis of the game and the struggle for the pennant.

Briol, Paul. The City of Rivers and Hills. Cincinnati, 1925. Fine description of the natural beauty of the city and some aspects of its history.

Burton, Gideon. Reminiscences of Gideon Burton. Cincinnati, 1895. Good background of late nineteenth century Cincinnati.

Chambrun, Clara Longworth. Cincinnati; Story of the Queen City. New York, 1939. History of Cincinnati from its pioneer days to 1939. It is a charming description of many aspects of the city's life.

Cincinnati. Bureau of Governmental Research. The Cincinnati Bureau of Municipal Research. Its First Year's Work. Cincinnati, 1910.

Cincinnati Enquirer. The Spirit of the New Cincinnati. Cincinnati, 1928. Fine descriptions of many aspects of the growing city.

Cincinnati Orphan Asylum. History of the Cincinnati Orphan Asylum, 1832-1882. . . Cincinnati, 1882. Includes an account of the fiftieth anniversary celebration of the orphan asylum.

Cincinnati's Institutions for Charity and Correction. A Complete Account of Their History, Their Purpose and Their Management. Cincinnati, 1899

Cincinnati Times-Star. 100th Anniversary Issue. Cincinnati, 1940.

Cist, Charles. Cincinnati in 1841: Its Early Annals and Future Prospects. Cincinnati, 1841.

────────── The Cincinnati Miscellany; or, Antiquities of the West and Pioneer History and General Local Statistics. . . Compiled from the Western General Advertiser October 1st 1844 to April 1st. . (1846). Cincinnati, 1845-46.

────────── Sketches and Statistics of Cincinnati in 1859. Cincinnati, 1859.

Comley, William J. and W. d'Eggville. Ohio: The Future Great State. Her Manufacturers and a History of Her Commercial Cities, Cincinnati and Cleveland, With Portraits and Biographies of Some of the Old Settlers, and Many of the Most Prominent Businessmen. Cincinnati, 1875.

Dabney, Wendell Phillips. Cincinnati's Colored Citizens; Historical, Sociological and Biographical. Cincinnati, 1926. Interesting analysis of the black population of the city and their contributions to its growth and development.

Dawson, James W. Picturesque Cincinnati. Cincinnati, 1883.

Day, Sarah J. The Man on a Hill Top. Philadelphia, 1931. Valuable biography of Timothy Day and his role in the growth of Cincinnati, a memorial to Sarah Day's father.

Drake, Benjamin and E.D. Mansfield. Cincinnati in 1826. Cincinnati, 1827. Fine description of all aspects of the city by one of its leading physicians.

Engelhardt, George Washington. Cincinnati, The Queen City. Cincinnati, 1901. History of the city from its founding through the nineteenth century.

Ferguson, E.A. Founding of the Cincinnati Southern Railway With an Autobiographical Sketch. Cincinnati, 1905.

Firemen's Protective Association, Cincinnati. History of the Cincinnati Fire Department, As Gleaned From all Available Sources of the History of Cincinnati From Its Earliest Incipiency, A.D. 1800 to A.D. 1895... and from Fire Department Records.... Cincinnati, 1895.

Ford, Henry A. and Mrs. K.B. Ford. History of Cincinnati, Ohio, With Biographical Sketches. Cincinnati, 1881.

Goldman, Robert P. An Analysis of Cincinnati's Proportional Representation Elections. Baltimore, 1930. This fine political study gives insights into Cincinnati's political life.

Goss, Charles Frederic. Cincinnati, the Queen City; 1788-1912. Chicago, 1912. 4 vols. A detailed history of the city is presented along with biographical sketches of its leading citizens.

Gray, Kenneth. A Report on Politics in Cincinnati. Cambridge, Massachusetts, 1959.

BIBLIOGRAPHY

Grove, Charles T. Centennial History of Cincinnati and Representative Citizens. Chicago, 1904. 2 vols. Presents a detailed analysis of the various aspects of life in Cincinnati.

Hall, Chester G., ed. The Cincinnati Southern Railway; A History. . . . Cincinnati, 1902.

Harlow, Alvin Fay. The Serene Cincinnatians. New York, 1950. Develops an interesting analysis of Cincinnati and her citizens.

Hurley, Edward Timothy. Cincinnati, Prints from the Etchings of E.T. Hurley. Cincinnati, 1916.

_____. The Town of the Beautiful River. Cincinnati, 1915.

Jublin, M. and Company. Cincinnati, Past and Present: Or, Its Industrial History, as Exhibited in the Life-Labors of Its Leading Men. Cincinnati, 1872.

King, Moses. King's Pocket-Book of Cincinnati. Cincinnati, 1840.

Klein, Benjamin Franklin. Life in Cincinnati at the Time of the Inauguration of each of the Presidents of the United States, as Copied from Newspapers of the Time. . . . Cincinnati, 1955.

Koch, Felix John. Cincinnati Sees It Through, The Camera's Story of How the Great World War Came to the Queen of the West. Cincinnati, 1917. This is an interesting set of photographs of the city in the early years of the First World War.

Leonard, John William. The Centennial Review of Cincinnati. 100 Years of Progress, in Commerce, Manufactures, the Professions, and in Social Municipal Life. Cincinnati, 1888.

Leonard, Lewis Alexander, ed. in chief. Greater Cincinnati and Its People; A History. New York, 1927. 4 vols. This is a fine series of essays on the history of Cincinnati and biographical sketches of its leading citizens.

Maxwell, Sidney Denise. The Suburbs of Cincinnati: Sketches, Historical and Descriptive. Cincinnati, 1870.

Mercfee, V. Worth. Cincinnati, Ohio, "the Queen City"; A Panoramic Portrayal of the Varied Activities and Interests of Cincinnati, Ohio. Cincinnati, 1926. Presents a fine descriptive account of the city.

Metzman, Gustav. Cincinnati and Ohio, Their Early Railroads. New York 1948.

Miles, Rufus E. The Cincinnati Bureau of Municipal Research. Philadelphia, 1912. Presents an account of the formation of this important branch of the city government.

Miller, Francis W. Cincinnati's Beginnings. Missing Chapters in the Early History of the City and the Miami Purchase Chiefly from Hitherto Unpublished Documents. Cincinnati, 1880.

Miller, Zane L. Boss Cox's Cincinnati: Urban Politics in the Progressive Era. New York, 1968. Presents a fine and valuable analysis of the era of the city boss of Cincinnati.

National Municipal League. Committee on Citizen's Charter Organization. The Cincinnati Plan of Citizen Organization for Political Activity. New York, 1934. This is a detailed analysis of the attempts of the citizens of Cincinnati to form a charter committee and how it worked in helping to reform city politics.

Nelson, S.B. and Company. History of Cincinnati and Hamilton County, Their Past and Present. Cincinnati, 1894.

Newspaper Cartoonists Association of Cincinnati. A Gallery of Pen Sketches in Black and White of "Cincinnatians As We See 'em." Cincinnati, 1905.

Norton, William J. The Social Unit Organization of Cincinnati. Cincinnati, 1919.

Park, Clyde William. The Cincinnati Equitable Insurance Company West of the Alleghenies. Cincinnati, 1954.

Perry, Dick. Vas You Ever in Zinzinnati? Garden City, New York, 1966. Presents an interesting and amusing account of the city.

Porter, Jermain G. Historical Sketch of the Cincinnati Observatory, 1843-1893. Cincinnati, 1893.

Powell, Lyman Pierson, ed. Historic Towns of the Western States. New York, 1901. An interesting analysis of Cincinnati and other cities is presented.

Prentis, Henning W. The Univeristy of Cincinnati. A Municipal University. Urbana, Illinois, 1919.

Reed, Doris D. The Cincinnati Area Must Solve Its Metropolitan Problems; A Report to the Stephen H. Wilder Foundation, Public Affairs Division. Cincinnati, 1953.

Reed, Thomas H. and Doris D. The Government of Cincinnati, 1924-1944; An Appraisal Report for Consultant Service of the National Municipal League, New York. Cincinnati, 1944.

Roe, George Mortimer, ed. Cincinnati: The Queen City of the West. Her Principal Men and Institutions. Biographical Sketches and Portraits of Leading Citizens. . . . Cincinnati, 1895.

Seasongood, Murray. Local Government in the United States; A Challenge and an Opportunity. Cambridge, Massachusetts, 1933. This is a series of lectures in which the author tells how he and others helped to reform the government of Cincinnati. It is a good study of government.

Shillito, John Company. Cincinnati. . . Past, Present and Future of Cincinnati. . . Cincinnati, 1888.

Smith, William C. Queen City Yesterdays; Sketches of Cincinnati in the Eighties. Crawfordville, Indiana, 1959. This is an interesting analysis of the decade of the 1880s.

Stevens, George F. The City of Cincinnati, Cincinnati, 1869.

Taft, Charles Phelps. City Management; The Cincinnati Experiment. New York, 1933. This is an interesting and enlightening analysis of the development of the City Manager form of government.

Teetor, Henry Benton. Sketch of the Life and Times of Colonel Israel Ludlow, one of the Original Proprietors of Cincinnati. Cincinnati, 1885.

Tucker, Louis Leonard. Cincinnati During the Civil War. Columbus, 1962. This is a good detailed study of the city's role during the Civil War.

_____. Cincinnati's Citizen Crusaders; A History of the Cincinnatus Association, 1920-1963. Cincinnati, 1967.

United States Works Progress Administration. Ohio. Tales of Old Cincinnati. Compiled by Workers of the Writers Program of the Work Projects Administration of the State of Ohio, 1940. Cincinnati, 1940. This is an interesting collection of legends.

United States Works Progress Administration. Ohio. They Built a City;

150 Years of Industrial Cincinnati. Compiled and Written by the Cincinnati Federal Writers' Project of the Works Progress Administration in Ohio. Cincinnati, 1938. Presents an interesting study of the city.

Wade, Richard C. The Urban Frontier. Chicago, 1964. A study of frontier life in Cincinnati and other cities.

Walters, Raymond W. Historical Sketch of the University of Cincinnati. Cincinnati, 1940.

———. Stephen Foster: Youth's Golden Dream; A Sketch of His Life and Background in Cincinnati, 1846-1850. Princeton, New Jersey, 1936. This is an account of the three years that Foster spent in Cincinnati working as a bookkeeper for a steamboat company when he began to write for Minstrel shows.

———. University of Cincinnati; Highlights, Past and Present. New York, 1952.

Williams, Caroline. The City on Seven Hills. Cincinnati, 1938. This is an excellent description of the city.

Wright, Henry C. Bossism in Cincinnati. Cincinnati, 1905. Presents an early account of boss rule in Cincinnati.

ARTICLES

Allen, Lee. "Baseball's Immortal Red Stockings," Historical and Philosophical Society of Ohio Bulletin, vol. XIX, July, 1961, 191-204.

Beckman, R.O. "How Cincinnati's New Government Is Improving Civil Service Morale," National Municipal Review, vol. XVIII, April, 1929, 232-236.

Bentley, H. "What Proportional Representation Has Done For Cincinnati," National Municipal Review, vol. XVIII, February, 1929, 65-67.

"Century Ago in the Schools of Cincinnati," Elementary School Journal, vol. XXX, May, 1930, 654-655.

"Cincinnati's Charter Commission," National Municipal Review, vol. VI, November, 1917, 720-722.

Drake, Daniel. Dr. Daniel Drake's Memoir of the Miami Country, 1779-1794 (an unfinished manuscript), ed. by Beverly W. Bond, Jr. Quarterly Publication of the Historical and Philosophical Society of Ohio, vol. XVIII, April-September, 1923.

BIBLIOGRAPHY

Drake, Daniel. "Notices Concerning Cincinnati," Quarterly Publication of the Historical and Philosophical Society of Ohio, vol. I, 1908, 1-60.

Garbutt, I.R. "Development of Cincinnati," Journal of Geography, vol. XIV, September, 1915, 10-12.

Henry, E.A. "Cincinnati as a Literary and Publishing Center, 1793-1880," Publishers' Weekly, No. 132, July 3-10, 1937, 22-24, 110-112.

Hessler, W.H. "Cincinnati: The City that Licked Corruption," Harper's Magazine, November, 1953, 76-81.

"Reform That Reformed Itself; Proportional-Representation Voting," The Reporter, vol. XVI, June 13, 1967, 20-24.

Lowrie, S.G. "Cincinnati's Charter Campaign," National Municipal Review, vol. III, October, 1914, 730-733.

Millard, W.J. "Why a New Government Was Proposed for Cincinnati," National Municipal Review, vol. XIII, November, 1924, 601-605.

Seasongood, Murray. "Triumph of Good Government in Cincinnati," Annals of the American Academy, vol. CXCIX, September, 1938, 83-90.

Seybold, G. "Dykstra of Cincinnati: Portrait of a Scholar in Action," Survey Graphic, vol. XXVI, April, 1937, 204-206.

Shepard, Lee. "When and By Whom, Was Cincinnati Founded?" Historical and Philosophical Society of Ohio Bulletin. vol. VII, 1949, 28-34.

Stern, Joseph S. "The Siege of Cincinnati," Historical and Philosophical Society of Ohio Bulletin, vol. XVIII, July, 1960, 163-186.

Stritch, Alfred G. "Political Nativism in Cincinnati, 1830-1860," Records of the American Catholic Historical Society of Philadelphia, vol. XLVII, 1937, 227-278.

Tafel, Mrs. Karl. "Early Cincinnati and the Turners," ed. by Leonard Koestler, Historical and Philosophical Society of Ohio Bulletin, vol. VII, January, 1949, 18-22.

Taft, Robert, Jr. "Epilogue of a Lady: The Passing of the Times-Star," Historical and Philosophical Society of Ohio Bulletin, vol. XVIII, October, 1960, 260-277.

Toppin, E.A. ."Humbly They Served: The Black Brigade in the Defense of

Cincinnati," The Journal of Negro History, vol. XLVIII, April, 1963, 75-97.

Wabritz, William S., ed. "The Bates Papers and Early Cincinnati," Historical and Philosophical Society of Ohio Bulletin, vol. XI, January, 1953, 13-36.

Wade, Richard C. "Negro in Cincinnati, 1800-1830," The Journal of Negro History, vol. XXXIX, January, 1954, 43-57.

Wilson, Charles R. "Cincinnati's Reputation During the Civil War," Journal of Southern History, vol. II, 1936, 468-479.

NAME INDEX

Adler, Henry, 34
Allison, Dr. Richard, 3
Arnold, Mrs. Brent, 44

Bachrach, Mayor Walton H., 61, 62, 63
Baker, Dr. A.H., 28
Bates, John, 18
Bauer, Miss B., 55
Baur, Miss Clara, 32
Bedini, Papal Nuncio, 25
Beecher, Rev. Lyman, 14, 16
Beecher, Catherine, 16
Beelor, J.A., 53
Bennett, George S., 20
Benson, Peter, 12
Berner, William, 41
Berry, Theodore M., 61
Bickel, Philip W., 27
Bigler, Dr. G.W., 25
Birney, James G., 18
Bishop, Mayor Richard M., 28
Black, Robert, 20
Blackman, Dr. George C., 31
Blaine, James G., 41
Buchanan, Joseph, 10
Buchta, Mayor G., 50
Bullock, Mrs. Sarah W., 38
Burnet, Dr., 3
Burnet, Mayor Isaac G., 13, 14
Burnett, Cornelius, 20

Caldwell, Mayor J.A., 45
Caldwell, James, 4
Caldwell, Judge, 50
Caldwell, Robert, 4
Calvin, Mayor John 50, 51
Canliffe, Calvin F., 65
Carnegie, Andrew, 46
Carry, Mayor William. 7
Cary, Alice, 26
Cash, Mrs., 60
Cash, Mayor Albert D., 58
Champion, Aaron G., 32
Clancy, Mayor Donald C., 61
Coffin, Levi, 23
Cohen, Alfred, 46
Conover, J.F., 18
Conover, James, 20
Cook, Theodore, 36
Cox, George B., 38, 42, 43, 44, 46, 47, 50
Cutler, Rev. Manasseh, 1

Dale, Frances, K., 63
Davidson, Tyler, 35
Davies, Mayor Samuel W., 16, 17, 18, 19
Davis, Mayor S.S., 34
Davis, Lieutenant Samuel B., 30
Dempsey, Governor Edward J., 47

Denman, Matthias, 1
Dolby, Mayor, 60
Drake, Benjamin, 12
Drake, Dr. Daniel, 4, 7, 9, 10, 17, 18, 24, 25
Draper, Dr. John, 32
Dykstra, Clarence A., City Manager, 55

Eckstein, Frederick, 12
Ehrman, Dr. B., 25
Eisenhower, President Dwight D., 60
Elder, Archbishop William Henry, 24, 47
Emery, Mrs. Thomas, 13

Faran, Mayor James J., 26
Fenwick, Rev. Edward, first Archbishop, 11, 15, 16
Filson, John, 1
Fleischmann, Mayor Julius, 46, 47
Flint, Timothy, 13
Foraker, Governor Joseph B., 42
Foster, Stephen, 22, 56

Gallagher, W.D., 18, 20
Gamble, J.N., 54
Gano, Gen. John S., 8
Garcia, H.A., 59
Gatchell, H.P., 25
George III, 1
Gibson, Mrs. Lauretta Bodman, 40
Godman, Dr. John D., 11
Goodman, T., 13
Grant, Ulysses S., III, 54
Grosbeck, William S., 36

Hammond, Charles, 18
Hannegan, Edward B., 5
Harmar, General, 2
Harper, William A., 18
Harrell, Charles Adair, City Manager, 60, 61
Harris, Mayor Leonard, 30, 31
Harrison, "Boy Preacher," 39
Harrison, Edmund, 8
Harrison, William Henry, 4
Hatch, Mayor George, 29
Haughton, R., 3
Hayes, Rutherford B., 30, 37
Hearst, William R., 50
Heidelbach, Espy, 30
Herron, Joseph, 22
Hine, Lucius, 23
Hopkins, Louis H., 31
Hotchkiss, Mayor Elisha, 15
Hughes, Thomas, 12
Hunt, Mayor Henry T., 49, 50

Ingalls, M.E., 47
Irwin, William, 7

Jacob, Mayor C., Jr., 38
Joliet, Louis, 1
Johnson, J. William, 32
Johnson, M., 63
Johnston, Mayor George W.C., 35, 36

Kellogg, Mr., City Manager, 60
Kelly, William C., 61
Kemper, Elnathan, 14
Kessler, George E., 47
Kidd, Captain John, 6
King, Edward, 16
King, John, 38
King, Rev. Martin Luther, Jr., 64
Kirk, William, 41
Klauprecht, Emil, 21
Koehler, Mayor Fred, 51

Lafayette, Marquis de, 12
Langdon, Elum P., 8
Laws, Miss Annie, 45
Lawson, Dr. Lemidas, 20, 21
Lilly, J.K., 56
Lincoln, Abraham, 26, 29, 30
Lincoln, Benjamin, 3
Lind, Jenny, 29
Locke, Dr., 11
Longworth, Nicholas, 20, 37
Longworth, Joseph, 37
Ludlow, Israel, 2
Ludlow, John, 2

McClain, William, Acting City Manager, 64
McFarland, William, 4
McLaughlin, Miss M. Louise, 38
McMiken, Charles, 33
McMillan, William, 2
McMurrich, Professor J.P., 52
Marquette, Pere Jacques, 1
Marshal, Dr., 20
Massey, Dr. W.H., 36
Mead, Dr., 25
Means, Mayor William R., 39
Menessier, Francis, 4
Miller, Dr. Adam, 25
Mitchell, Ormsby, 20
Moeller, Archbishop Henry, 47
Moore, R.M., 38
Morehead, John, 17
Morgan, John, 30
Mosby, Mayor John, 43, 44
Murray, Miss Annie, 43

Nabokov, Vladimir, 61
Nash, Arthur, 53

Newman, Henry F., 41
Nichols, George Ward, 35
North, Dr. E.E., 51

Osborn, Dr. Mary Elizabeth, 43

Page, Colonel, 51
Palmer, Joseph, 41
Parsons, General Samuel H., 1
Parvin, Dr. Theophilus, 31
Patterson, Col. Robert, 1
Peaslee, John B., 43
Perkins, James H., 21
Peter, Mrs. Sarah Worthington King, 26, 28
Pickering, Timothy, 3
Pittman, Benn, 26
Probasco, Henry, 35
Proctor, Mr., 47
Pulte, Joseph H., 25
Purcell, Dr. John Baptist, Bishop and then Archbishop, 16, 20, 24
Putnam, Gen. Rufus, 1

Randolph, Beverly, 3
Reeder, Jesse, 8
Reemlin, Charles, 18
Rhodes, Governor James A., 63
Rice, Rev. David, 2
Rich, Mayor Carl W., 58, 59, 60
Rigers, Dr. John, 11
Ruehlmann, Mayor Eugene P., 64, 65

Sage, Dr. F.W., 41
St. Clair, General Arthur, 1, 2
Samuels, Mrs. T.B., 53
Schmidlapp, Jacob G., 54

Schneller, Fred, 54
Schwab, Mayor Louis, 49
Scott, General Winfield, 29
Seasongood, Mayor Murray, 53
Selman, Robert, 11
Semple, Mrs., 62
Shaw, Robert, 2
Shattler, Dr. Robert, 44
Sherrill, Col. Clarence, first City Manager, 53, 55, 56
Shinley, Murray, 31
Slack, Elijah, 10
Smith, Mayor Amor, Jr., 41
Snellbaker, Mayor David T., 26
Spencer, Mayor Henry F., 21
Spencer, Rev. O.M., 7
Spiegel, Mayor Friedrich S., 50
Springer, Reuben R., 36, 37
Stanton, Edwin M., 26
Stephens, Mayor T.J., 40
Stevens, Dr. E.B., 38
Stewart, Mayor James Garfield, 56, 57, 58
Stites, Benjamin, 1
Stone, Ethan, 7
Storer, Mrs. Maria Longworth, 39
Stowe, Harriet Beecher, 16
Struder, Dr., 20
Stubbs, Robert, 4
Symmes, John Cleves, 1, 2

Tafel, Mayor Gustav, 45
Taft, Mrs. Alphonso, 38
Taft, Mayor Charles Phelps, 52, 54, 61
Taft, Mrs. Charles Phelps, 52, 54, 55

Taft, William Howard, 38, 45
Talliafero, Dr., 20
Taylor, Eli, 18
Taylor, Mayor Mark P., 25
Thacker, Dr. J.A., 33
Thomas, E.S., 18
Thomas, Frederick, 18
Thomas, Mayor Nicholas W., 27
Thorpe, Dr. Juliet Monroe, 43
Thrasher, Dr. A.B., 41
Torrence, Mayor John F., 33

Van Buren, Martin, 17
Vattier, Dr., 20

Wales, Prince of, 29
Waldvogel, Mayor, 59, 60
Walker, Timothy, 16
Waterman, Fred, 32
Wayne, Gen. "Mad" Anthony, 3
West, Charles W., 39
White, James, 3
Withorne, F., 55
Wichman, William C., City Manager, 64
Williams, Peter, 6
Williams, Sydney, 60
Willson, Mayor Russell, 56
Wilson, Dr., 35
Wilson, Woodrow, 53
Wilstach, Mayor Charles F., 32
Winton, Mathew, 4
Wise, Dr. Isaac, 20, 34, 37
Woodward, William, 12
Wright, Harry, 32
Wright, John C., 16

Yeatman, Griffin, 3, 4